THE WITNESSES

One God, One Victory

Chandler W. Sterling

HENRY REGNERY COMPANY • CHICAGO

Library of Congress Cataloging in Publication Data

Sterling, Chandler W   Bp., 1911—
    The Witnesses.

    1. Jehovah's Witnesses.   I.   Title.
BX8526.S73   289.9   74-26874
ISBN 0-8092-8448-0

Published by Henry Regnery Company
180 North Michigan Avenue, Chicago, Illinois 60601
Manufactured in the United States of America
Library of Congress Catalog Card Number: 74-26874
International Standard Book Number: 0-8092-8448-0

Published simultaneously in Canada by
Fitzhenry & Whiteside Limited
150 Lesmill Road
Don Mills, Ontario M3B 2T5
Canada

The putting together and writing of this book was accomplished at the Lindisfarne Community. In order not to interfere with the day-to-day routine necessities of teaching, learning, meditating, and sharing in the total community life, it meant doing the typescript in the early morning hours. To all my colleagues I dedicate this book, especially to those whose rooms adjoined mine at the end of the corridor whose unwanted alarm clock was my typewriter.

Lindisfarne,
Southampton, Long Island, N.Y.
June 21, 1974

Contents

Preface

There is one rather large group of people for whom the threat of continuing wars, or an atomic holocaust, means very little. They feel no anxiety over the doings of men or the cataclysms of nature. They have learned to live with some serenity through the trials and deterioration of the nation-states. Actually, they look forward toward the time when any one of these catastrophes might be totally fulfilled. They receive considerable private pleasure out of anticipating the final collapse of the works of man—and Satan. They further believe that such a major event in the world of men or nature, or both, will prove to be the last upheaval before Armageddon. It would be regarded as the curtain-raiser to the dramatic descent from heaven of the armies of angels sent here by the wrathful command of an angry Jehovah to destroy the last Babylon, twentieth-century society.

These convictions are based upon grim predictions in the

book of Revelation in Christian Scripture, which declare that Har-ma-ged-on will be the last battle between good and evil. The Witnesses are counting on Armageddon, as it has come to be called. Their eager expectation is fortified by the conviction that they alone will be the sole survivors of this terrible cataclysm.

While there are other groups, and individual persons, who share the millennial expectations of the Witnesses, these people alone believe that once the forces of evil have been finally overthrown, then they themselves will live in joy and plenty forever on an altogether perfect earth, a miraculously restored Eden. They do not expect any post-cataclysmic crisis of living on berries and bark or what might be salvaged from the ruins of supermarkets. They have no fear of huddling in caves or city ruins in the post-atomic jungle. Although nobody seems certain or very specific about it, they expect the earth to be free from famine, plague, pestilence, and war. Moreover, there will no longer be any annoying insects, poisonous plants, reptiles, dangerous beasts, or great extremes in climate. The only place in the picture that is unpleasant is that the surviving and spared Witnesses will have to stand aside as the angels of the Lord do the killing for them, leaving the elect to a seven-month task of burying the dead. After that has been accomplished, the thousand-year reign of peace will begin.

Another startling fact about these people is that every single one of them is a practicing minister, either on a full-time or a part-time basis. They are also always ready to brave the scorn, contempt, and abuse of hostile and unsympathetic people who look down upon them as "religious nuts." Yet they are a quiet and peace-loving people. They are also pavement-pounding missionaries, house-to-house proselytizers. They are dogged stair-climbers and compulsive doorbell pushers. The zeal that they show in spreading the word that the end of all things is at hand sometimes leads to conversions and at other times to violence. In America, these people have been stoned, and their private homes and places of meeting burned. Some of them in the not distant past have been tarred, feathered, and run out of town. Many have been murdered. Others lost their lives in Dachau and the Nazi prison camps, where they died for their faith. Their reaction to all of these sufferings has been to get back up on their feet and proceed to the next house.

But surely the most astonishing fact about the Jehovah's Witnesses is that they are the fastest growing religious body in the world. At a time when the churches are showing a statistical decline, or at best a one or two percent gain during the past twenty-five years, the Jehovah's Witnesses show an honest gain of 2,300 percent! The Witnesses can claim more than one million four hundred thousand members in 203 countries, and 5,492 congregations. The Jehovah's Witnesses are a modern-day miracle of growth and expansion. Fifty years ago, there were fewer than 3,000 members of the Society. In 1940, there were barely 17,000. Today, in the United States alone, there are over 431,000 members.

In an age of dying churches and organizational forms of the familiar culture-religions, the Witnesses are very much alive, burgeoning and juggernauting their way through American society. A century and more ago, the Mormons, under Brigham Young, stated that they were going west to get away from the state and church. They were temporarily successful in these aims. The Witnesses endure the state and ignore the churches, showing every sign that they are going to be around for awhile—at least until Armageddon and then some—but not the rest of us.

Every sign of cultural break-up in our day is regarded as good news by the Witnesses, for it signifies the end of all

things and the final delay of Jehovah, who has had quite
enough of humanity by now to where He is at the point of
closing out the entire operation—except for His Witnesses.
Here is the story of an intent and expectant people confidently awaiting the final manifestation of their Jehovah
God, now ready to roll up the scroll of time.

1

The Remnant of Revelation

The modern Babylon now sits, and rules men to their harm.
Almost all men she has enchained within her mystic charm.
With lying lips and cunning ways, she wields a mighty power,
Deceiving all within her realm, in this her final hour.

There is a recurrent theme in the history of religions. It always begins with an elite, a small group—clique if you will—of men and women who are honestly trying to live a less worldly life than their neighbors. These persons have drawn together in their attempts to be more attentive to the directly felt guidance of the spirit. Gradually they draw apart from all other religionists, a hive ready to swarm, hovering in anticipation of the great dance around the queen, the idea, or the leader.

From outside observers there are ridiculous and snide jokes on over-godliness. There are frequent stupid and cruel acts of repression. Sometimes there is persecution by insensitive and unsympathetic authorities. There is always the contempt of the half-Christian, or the half-anything for that matter. This is complete with the usual trite references to old wine and new bottles, the kernel and the husk, and the like.

Invariably the enthusiastic new movement is denounced as an innovation as it firmly insists that it is actually either preserving or restoring the primitive discipline of the Church or institution. There are many people who do not relish what they consider an eccentric spirituality. They find themselves immediately in an unwelcome and unsought-after alliance with worldlings who do not relish any kind of spirituality whatsoever. The Witnesses repeat this feeling and experience every day.

Almost always, schism begets schism. Growth by fission is characteristic. Although there has been defection, as one should expect, yet they have not become a divided body. A movement tends to breed rival prophets. With the exception of a brief flurry during the ascendancy of Judge Rutherford to the position of successor and leader to Charles Taze Russell the movement somehow has been able to avoid rivalries and power struggles. Its internal unity has been threatened only once in its history.

While it is true that the first fervors evaporate, these people have managed to generate new enthusiasms through slight and occasional changes in the body of faith such as new explanations of further delayed and yet unfulfilled predictions. Usually prophecy dies out. Finally, the charismatic is merged with the institutional. The "high that proved too high, the heroic for earth too hard," is the fugue that runs through the story of mankind, his ideas, aspirations, and deeds. Still, the Witnesses stay doggedly to the dream of faith.

The Jehovah's Witness expects more evidence of God's grace than outside people do. He cannot tolerate any "almost-Witnesses." There is no place for weaker brethren. There are no Witnesses that are in the process of accepting the faith. Either one receives it in full or one does not have any of it at all. There is no place in Kingdom Hall for the one who plods and stumbles over problems of faith. If one's ambition is simply to qualify and not to excel, then he is regarded as not worthy of his calling. It is as simple as that.

The Witness has before his eyes at all times a picture of the Church as he believes it to have been in its earlier days and more primitive stages. He looks upon this pristine elite as being visibly penetrated and saturated with super-natural influences that were so strong that Jehovah relented and, with some reluctance, apparently postponed Armageddon again and again. One osmotically receives the idea that there are times when Jehovah finds certain men irresistible. The Witness can never be satisfied with a lesser vision than this. The irresistible total 144,000 down through the years, and this figure obviously does not include *all* Witnesses. Indeed, we shall discover that the list does not even include all the Old Testament worthies, the sages and prophets of old.

In speaking of such matters—and it is difficult to discuss such subjects with a Witness—an exception to what he accepts as truth simply cannot be true. There are no "yes, but—" considerations for him. This is when he will part company with you. To him there is not the slightest possibility of an exception, interpretation, or accommodation. There are no such things as extenuating circumstances in belief. Therefore, there can be none about the most sacred calf of all, Armageddon.

He can quote a hundred selected texts and reject a thousand others to the contrary. By these he can insist that the members of this Society are saved members from a perishing world and that they are especially called to lead a life of angelic purity and apostolic simplicity. Worldly amusements are the traps of a polite and sophisticated society. A Witness makes his way around these as though he were crossing a mined field. Any lapse that occurs produces a yield of scandal within the body that results in the rejection of the sinner. Sometimes he is restored after sufficient contrition and amendment of life has been demonstrated to the congregation. But with a reluctant and suspicious absolution it takes an exceptionally strong person in both courage and faith to return to the fold. Even backsliders rarely regain their former status as devout believers.

The thrust of the movement depends mainly on the belief that they have a direct, personal access to the Author of salvation. Intellectual girding is regarded as generally unnecessary. It is certainly minimized. Liturgical expression is totally missing. The singing of "spiritual songs" (not called hymns) has been an innovation of only twenty-five years back. During Rutherford's reign singing was regarded as frivolous.

The Witness believes that he has emerged into a new order of being. One suspects that if he believed in Darwin's theory of evolution, he could regard himself as Jehovah's final product, the apotheosis of piety. He feels that he has a new set of faculties that have come into his possession through Jehovah because he has been called out of this world—to live in it, but not of it. He generally deplores the use of reason beyond his prescribed studies. All of it is unnecessary, especially to a Witness, because a direct indication of the Divine Mind and Will is given to him and his brethren only.

These elect of God, being required by the circumstances of life to live and work alongside unbelievers and the sons of perdition, regard it as the road that they must travel. He has another citizenship than that of his associate on the job, who cannot possibly survive Armageddon. The Witness will submit himself to *almost,* but not quite, every ordinance and law of Caesar. He always does so under vigorous protest. He insists that worldly governments and nation-states have no mandate from anybody—let alone Jehovah—to govern anybody. Yet, the fancied rights of the state must be accepted, *except* in certain instances. He believes devoutly in his heart that the anomalies of the present situation will soon be done away with. The righteous shall gain the rule in the very near and foreseeable future as Armageddon plods steadily toward the climax and the end of time.

2

The Millennial Yearnings of Charles Taze Russell

Little is known of the early days of the unique and attractive founder of the Society that in later years became known as the Jehovah's Witnesses. The movement had been active and working for more than forty years before the present name was given to the Society. Charles Taze Russell was a diminutive man with an ascetic and kindly manner and appearance. As he grew older, his patriarchal bearing was further emphasized by long white hair and a flowing white beard. He spent nearly fifty years of his life warning the world of its imminent end.

It seems likely that the claims are true that Russell was unable to attend college because of his responsibilities to the family business. He had ample means at his disposal to do so, for he and his father owned and operated five clothing stores in cities around Pittsburgh, Pennsylvania.

In his young manhood Charles Russell was a pious and orthodox member of the Presbyterian Church in

Allegheny, Pennsylvania. But as a boy in his early teens he felt so strongly about the prevailing doctrine of predestination and the harsh Calvinism of nineteenth-century Appalachia and God's consignment of sinners to an eternal hell, that he went around town writing scriptural passages on walks, walls, and the sides of buildings, that all who passed might heed the possible loss of their own souls.

The small-town pool hall was an integral part of American culture in the last half of the nineteenth century. It was the social hub of every village, uninvaded by the fair sex. Even though one did not play pool or billiards after he discovered for himself that he did not have the talent for such serious and deadly earnest frivolities, it still remained the place where you met your friends for whatever was being planned for the evening by the town's young blades. Charles Taze Russell was one of them, a most attractive and pleasing one at that.

One evening he roved into a local pool hall to idle away a few moments. He became engaged, by his own account, in a conversation that finally centered on various subjects in the Bible and came to rest on the Protestant doctrine of hell. This is not to be regarded as unusual or improbable, for in the eighteen seventies and as late as the eighties these were common and unselfconscious topics of discussion in public. As a fundamentalist Christian, young Russell tried in vain to defend the doctrine. He lost the argument amid great embarrassment. That was the last confrontation that Charles Taze Russell ever admitted losing.

After the trauma of defeat had subsided, he was unable to forget this experience, which he took, at the tender age of eighteen, as a personal insult and humiliation. He thereupon set himself the task of examining the biblical foundation for belief in hell—particularly the hot variety. While in this crisis of belief, Russell had parted company with the Presbyterians and joined the Congregational Church, as it was known in that day. However, he began his studies on his own. In those days the only material on the subject was that which could be found in Holy Scripture. He called his original investigation an "examination done with the logic of infidelity." Presumably this is meant to explain that he approached the problem from the point of view of the critical and searching believer.

For his time this should be regarded as remarkable, for the new methodology of science sired by Darwin and Huxley had scarcely been born. Here Russell was using a new tool—the critical and agnostic approach to a biblical problem. Since these days the great universities of Oxford and Cambridge, as well as those in Germany and other places on the continent, began their inquiry into the validity of Christian doctrine. But this young man was required to do his private study against discouraging odds. He did not have a teacher—except the Lord and Spirit, as he said. There was no one to lead him across the no man's land of biblical exegesis, itself still in its infancy. He also suffered from a lack of academic background and education. He had nobody to direct his rather remarkable talents in his desperate and thorough search for the truth.

In a 1906 issue of *The Watchtower*, Charles Taze Russell recounts and reminisces about his young manhood in the late eighteen sixties and early seventies:

> Let me begin the narrative at the year 1868 when the Editor [Russell himself] having been a consecrated child of God for some years, and a member of the Congregational Church and the Young Men's Christian Association, began to be shaken in faith regarding many long-accepted doctrines. Brought up a Presbyterian, and indoctrinated from the catechism and being naturally

of an inquiring mind, I fell an easy prey to the logic of infidelity as soon as I began to think for myself. But that which at first threatened to be the utter shipwreck of faith in God and the Bible was, under God's providence, overruled for good, and merely wrecked my confidence in human creeds and systems of misrepresentation of the Bible.

Gradually I was led to see that the thought of each of the creeds contained some elements of truth, they were on the whole misleading and contradictory to God's word. Among other theories I stumbled upon Adventism. Seemingly by accident one evening, I dropped into a dusty, dingy hall where I heard religious services were being held to see if the handful who met there had anything more sensible to offer than the creeds of the great churches. There, for the first time, I heard something of the views of Second Adventism, the preacher being Mr. Jonas Wendell, a long-since deceased sailor and former Baptist. Though his Scripture expositions were not entirely clear, and though it was very far from what we rejoice in, it was sufficient under God to re-establish my wavering faith in the divine inspiration and to show that the records of the apostles and prophets are indissolubly linked.

The group of Adventists that Russell referred to was founded by a William Miller in 1829. Their principal belief was that the Second Coming of Jesus would happen in 1844. When this did not come about, the cult broke up. It is quite likely that this was a remnant group of "Millerites" that Russell came across on that fateful spring evening. He became convinced eventually that they were the precursors of his movement somewhat as John the Baptist preceded Jesus' ministry. The reason why all this seems plausible and probable is because the Millerites, or Adventists, as they became known, were the only congregation that Russell never condemned. As we are about to discover for ourselves, that is saying a great deal.

At the time of this chance meeting and acquaintance with the Adventist movement, fragmented as it was, young Russell was deep in his inquiry into Scripture. After painful, intensive, and prolonged searching of the Bible, he concluded that hell was nonexistent—certainly in the sense that the preachers described it. In the forming years that lay ahead the first of his followers were known as the "no-hell" people in a world full of brimstone believers. They were laughed at and ridiculed for "turning the hose on hell," as one wit described Russell's teaching on the subject. In later years he would ask, while preaching, "Would you hold a puppy dog's tail in a fire for even three minutes?" Then he would answer the rhetorical question, "Of course not—unless you were sub-human. Yet we are taught that God consigns creatures to everlasting tortures in fire hotter than any we can imagine."

Russell wasn't exactly making friends with prominent churches or their leaders in that day; nevertheless he discovered himself being propelled toward reactionary religious cults that were forming as they proclaimed the end of the world, or at best, the Second Coming. He was the sole motivating force in the group that he founded. He possessed a natural charm, presence, and winsomeness. His reputed broad-mindedness on second sight generally proved to be a sort of benevolent and benign bull-headedness and pleasant obstinacy. Both his extreme claims and his exclusive devotion to the Bible drew disciples to his feet. He had what we call so loosely today *charisma,* the "light touch" that made it easy for people to draw toward him and identify with him. He always had time for everybody. He always consented to have his picture taken, oftentimes at great inconvenience, for his travel and speaking tours were tightly scheduled. This man of slight stature, with a saintly aura about him, in later life contributed the patriarchal glow and appearance to his person that is so memorable through his portraits and photographs. In his speech, both public and private, he was a spellbinder. But most of all, he was a kindly man. And as St. Paul said of Barnabas, so too, could one say of Charles Taze Russell:

. . . he was a good man and full of holy spirit and of faith .
—Acts 11:24, NWT*

Charles Russell may not have been surprised by his discoveries, but he was impressed when he perceived that the records of the Apostles of the New Testament and the Gospels are indissolubly linked with the prophets of the Old Testament and that there might indeed be a tangible succession in history to these earlier men of God. From this point he investigated the various doctrines of the millennial and Adventist sects and their individual understanding, interpreting, and application of Scripture. He concluded in characteristic Russell fashion that they had not read the records right. Therefore, he set about making his own computation to figure out an accurate date for the Second Coming.

He felt his way through the labyrinth of Scripture. The turning point in his thought, and the establishment of his base for calculations, was when he read and examined that part of the New Testament that is known to biblical

---

*The *New World Translation of the Holy Scriptures* (NWT) is the Jehovah's Witnesses authorized version of the Bible.

scholars and students as the "Little Apocalypse." This lengthy passage appears in its earliest form in the New Testament in Mark 13:1-37. It is enlarged, glossed, and editorialized in Matthew 24:1-51 and in Luke 21:5-36. While these are separate and similar accounts obviously written for different kinds of readers of varied cultural backgrounds, principally Jews, Romans, and Greeks, respectively, it is generally accepted that in Mark is the oldest account. Both the writers of the Gospels of Matthew and Luke apparently drew upon this source for their versions, which are more detailed and considerably more colorful and descriptive. Russell, unaware probably of the burgeoning Oxford and Cambridge schools of biblical scholarship and the development of the new methodology as applied to ancient writings, made his unique discoveries completely on his own. He had no teachers.

We don't know today whether Russell began his reading of the New Testament in the conventional manner of starting with the Gospel of Matthew, wading laboriously through the "begats," and thence to Mark, Luke, and the other books. Being of a pietistic nature, he probably read the New Testament books in the order in which they appear in the Bible.

It is in Matthew's version of the "Little Apocalypse" that one first comes across the reference to the Book of Daniel:

> Therefore, when you catch sight of the disgusting thing that causes desolation, as spoken of through Daniel the prophet, standing in a holy place, (let the reader use discernment,) then let those in Judea begin fleeing to the mountains.
>
> —Matthew 24:15, NWT

There is also a reference in Mark:

> However, when you catch sight of the disgusting
> thing that causes desolation standing where it
> ought not (let the reader use discernment), then
> let those in Judea begin fleeing to the mountains.
>
> —Mark 13:14, NWT

The Gospel of Luke deals with the passage and subject differently:

> Furthermore, when you see Jerusalem surround-
> ed by encamped armies, then know that the
> desolating of her has drawn near. Then let those
> in Judea begin fleeing to the mountains, and let
> those in the midst of her withdraw, and let those
> in the country places not enter into her; because
> these are days for meting out justice, that all the
> things written may be fulfilled.
>
> —Luke 21:20-24, NWT

The balance of the "Little Apocalypse" is quoted here directly from the New World Translation:

> Woe to the pregnant women and the ones suck-
> ling a baby in those days! For there will be great
> necessity upon the land and wrath on this peo-
> ple; and they will fall by the edge of the sword
> and be led captive into all the nations; and
> Jerusalem will be trampled on by the nations,
> until the appointed times of the nations are
> fulfilled. Also, there will be signs in sun and
> moon and stars, and on the earth anguish of
> nations, not knowing the way out because of the
> roaring of the sea and [its] agitation, while men
> become faint out of fear and expectation of the

things coming upon the inhabited earth; for the
powers of the heavens will be shaken. And then
they will see the Son of man coming in a cloud
with power and great glory. But as these things
start to occur, raise yourselves erect and lift your
heads up, because your deliverance is getting
near.

—Luke 21:23-28, NWT

In the passage above, "until the appointed times of the
nations are fulfilled" is the key to Russell's prophecy. He
proceeded from there by figuring that "the times of the
Gentiles must have commenced when Nebuchadnezzar
overthrew Jerusalem." (The reason for the use of the word
"Gentiles" here, instead of the word "nations" [in the
Luke text above] is due to the fact that Russell had only
the King James Version of the Bible available to him. The
New World Translation did not appear until after Russell's
time.)

Secular historians place this date at 586 B.C.E. Russell,
however, characteristically applied his operational principle of unorthodoxy to historical as well as spiritual and
scriptural matters. Accordingly, he placed the date in October of 607 B.C.E. This date becomes the key year
backwards and forwards in his reckonings.

From this passage in Luke, Russell went back to
Leviticus and Daniel in the Old Testament, feeling his way
painstakingly through the biblical maze. He learned from
these sources that Israel was to suffer seven times for its
sins. He decided on his own at this point that this *must* be
the "times of the Gentiles" referred to by Jesus in Luke
21:24. Then he was off on the hunt for the meaning of "the
times."

This was not accomplished quickly because what he was

searching for was in a passage near the end of Scripture in Revelation:

> But the two wings of the great eagle were given the woman, that she might fly into the wilderness to her place; there is where she is fed for a time and times and half a time away from the face of the serpent.
>
> —Revelation 12:14, NWT

Through this method of spot-checking, Russell saw clearly, as far as he himself was concerned, that twelve hundred and sixty days are "a time and times and half a time." It added up in his calculations to the figure 1260 days, which comes out to seven years, which is what "twice that many days" means.

The spot-check method of picking one's way through the cave of Scripture can produce disastrous results, of course. But the method is not regarded as absurd by the Witnesses. Indeed, it is highly doubtful that it has even occurred to them that a spot-check method of determining what is true, and sometimes to divine the future, is a risky business.

To support the Witness approach, one may cite the conversion of St. Augustine in the third century. He records the shaking event in his *Confessions*:

> So I was moved to return to the place where Alypius was sitting, for I had put down the Apostle's book [Epistle to the Romans] there when I arose. I snatched it up, opened it, and in silence read the first passage upon which my eyes fell:
>
> > "Let us walk honestly, as in the day;
> > not in rioting and drunkenness, not in

chambering and wantonness, not in
strife and envying. But put ye on the
Lord Jesus Christ, and make not provi-
sion for the flesh, to fulfil the lusts
thereof."
(Romans 13:13-14, King James Version)

I had no wish to read further, and no need. For in
that instant . . . it was as though a light of utter
confidence shown in all my heart and the
darkness of uncertainty vanished away.
—St. Augustine, *Confessions,* Chapter 13

Now, if one of the greatest minds the historic church has
ever produced used this method to discern the will of God,
then why not anyone?

Russell engaged himself with much figuring in his individual and lonely attempt to unravel Scripture, twisting
and wrenching from it the truth he sought that seemed so
obscure and hidden within from even the earnest seeker.
He endured the handicaps of being without an education, a
teacher or guide, or any of the tools necessary for an inquiry
into Scripture. He was only temporarily discouraged when
he realized that the first figure he came up with had the Second Coming happening six hundred years before the first.
Undaunted, he returned to the enigma and the puzzle-
maze of the Bible convinced that he was at fault, that he
had overlooked something important that lay hidden in the
lush growth of words, something expectantly subtle that
would provide the key that would unlock the secret of how
long the world must continue on its present course before
the final divine intervention. He personally continued the
search for his personal tetragrammaton, reading and
studying by himself. Finally, he came across a passage in
Ezekiel that reads:

A day for a year, a day for a year, is what I have
given you.

—Ezekiel 4:6, NWT

Charles Taze Russell now could see that "seven times"
should be twenty-five hundred and twenty *years* instead of
days. (He dropped off the months of November and
December of the year 607 in his earlier chronological ad-
justment. This is how he arrived at the year 1914 as the
date for the Second Coming. All of this figuring and ad-
justing was accomplished by Russell in 1874.)

What had started Russell off on this search for the date
of the end of all things was that he believed that William
Miller, the founder of Adventism, had the right idea but
that his calculations were off. Miller had figured that the
Lord would return in the early eighteen forties, probably
1843 or 1844. Russell was born in 1852, and by 1870 had
begun following the millennial trail. What had happened
to Miller was amazing. Thousands joined his movement.
People deserted Methodism and Presbyterianism.
Disciples and Baptists also flocked to him. These days
came and went. Nothing having happened, his converts
fell away. Only a handful stayed with him and held on to
their belief that the Day had been only briefly delayed. It
was one of these remnant groups that Russell had come
across in his evening wanderings about town while on his
father's business in retail men's clothing. (The center remnant of Miller's Adventist group continued under a
prophetess, Ellen G. White. However, she incorporated the
observance of Saturday Sabbath, plus various health and
dietary regulations, into a church that is known today as
the Seventh-Day Adventist Church.)

Believing that he had discovered the flaw in Miller's
figures of thirty years past, Russell published his own interpretation of the *invisible* Second Coming. This was called

The Object and Manner of the Lord's Return (1873). His father paid the printing bill. Money was never a problem in Charles Russell's life, because of his happy family circumstances. He never had a financial struggle in the development and promulgation of his ideas. This was indeed a happy circumstance for a person who had had a vision, for there were no foundations to apply to for aid in that day. Russell did not need financial aid beyond that which his father generously produced. His father was apparently quite proud of his gentle and pious son with the probing and inquisitive spiritual nature. He supported Charles throughout his entire life and maintained that loving relationship.

As Russell went about the east coast on business trips, he came across a magazine, *Herald of the Morning*, published by the Adventists. In looking it over, he discovered that the editor also believed that Jesus had already returned to earth as an invisible angel—in the year 1874—and that mankind was already in the early stages of the millennium. This was gratifying to this lonely reader, curious and concerned about such things. He made contact with this editor immediately. The man, N. H. Barbour, was also a printer by trade. Russell put some of his money into the magazine. Later on, when Russell sold out his business interest in the family clothing chain, he became co-editor.

Within three years—by the time he was twenty-five—Russell called a meeting of the clergy of the prominent and influential parishes of Pittsburgh. Many of them accepted his invitation to meet with him. The host, in his sincere, honest, and naive way, proceeded to explain to his guests that he received a new understanding of the invisible Second Coming. He was most disappointed to have his enthusiastic and enlightening discoveries rejected by this august group. Without exception they returned to their congregations and resumed the spinning of their own theological webs. It is hard for us to imagine today that Russell actually believed that he could sway his clergy guests toward an immediate belief in his self-taught theories about Scripture and what it purportedly had to say about date-setting the millennium. For the rest of his life, from that point on, he had nothing but bitter feelings toward the clergy of any and all churches—except the Adventist people. His first humiliation was in the pool hall with the trauma of the lost argument and his defeat at the hands of a billiard player. His second humiliation was at the hands of his condescending guests. Now his public embarrassment came to an end.

He had become so involved in his scriptural investigations and studies, and his writing about them, that he sold out his business interests completely for a figure in excess of $250,000. He was now free and financed to devote all of his time to the cause, preaching in the rare and scattered places where he had been invited. He organized Bible classes everywhere he went. Within the year he and Barbour wrote a book together called *The Three Worlds, or the Plan of Redemption.* In it were explained the methods they used whereby they calculated that the Second Coming had already happened in 1874, three years prior to the publication of the book in 1877. This date of the Invisible Second Coming was the beginning of the countdown that would eventually end with the times of the Gentiles in 1914.

Although it was hardly apparent to either Russell or Barbour during their short time together that they were on a collision course, the inevitable did happen. The precipitating cause was a disagreement over the meaning of the ransom that Jesus paid. Barbour's view was regarded by Russell as a heresy, and he tried to insert articles in the magazine that would contradict Barbour. The partnership was dissolved and they went their separate ways.

With capital now available, Russell started up his own magazine, which appeared first in July of 1879. He called it *The Watch Tower and Herald of Christ's Presence.* The first issue was for 6,000 copies.

3

"A Good Man and Full of the Holy Spirit"—the Society under Pastor Russell

This intense young man possessed a degree of self-confidence that was impressive, to say the least. Starting out in his biblical studies with no knowledge of Hebrew, Greek, or Latin (except what he could learn for himself with a dictionary), he took on the entire field of biblical scholarship—including the learned men from Cambridge, Oxford, and the continent, giants whose learning and accomplishments were outstanding. They were a formidable lot who were somewhat impressed with each other's learning, thus producing an intellectual elite that found it easy to bully benignly any and all lesser opponents. One wonders at times whether it ever occurred to Russell that Scripture had already received a rather thorough combing out and investigation during these days of the Darwinian revolution. Commentaries and books on scriptural subjects were easily available. Russell seems to have been blissfully unaware of the late nineteenth-century activity among biblical scholars who were working in the newly developing fields of Biblical Criticism, Higher Criticism, *Formgeschichte,* and the new biblical archaeology. He lived in the days of great academic ferment over the questions of authority and validity of Scripture—a ferment that was precipitated anew by the work of Darwin and Huxley. There is no indication whatever that he ever knew that such inquiry was already going on at the highest academic level.

Many of the biblical doctrines that distressed him also distressed the biblical scholars of that day. In a way, they were on his side, though neither realized it. They were also doing study and investigation. They had the inestimable advantage of having a classical education in their background, plus a firm grounding in Latin, Greek, and Hebrew as well as the Arabic languages. Yet one wonders whether the knowledge of the existence of the information that Russell was seeking would have modified any of his conclusions, which he deduced from his own private studies.

He seems to have developed a practice of approaching each and every biblical problem as though he were solving a jigsaw puzzle. He would lay out each verse and text on a table, so to speak, as a person would lay out a puzzle for solution containing as many as a thousand pieces. Russell did something like this, although he soon restricted the texts. From the final selection he would attempt to put together what seemed to him to be a true and reasonable picture of the books of both Daniel and Revelation.

Persons interested in millennialism and the cataclysmic end of the world use the books of Daniel and Revelation as their authority source. The literary style of these two books is called "apocalyptic." Besides the use of highly colorful and dramatic language, this style is saturated with symbolism. Numbers, figures, and archetypes from astrology, numerology, and the ancient "arts of the Chaldeans" are profuse.

The Christian inquirer into millennialism and its eschatology would begin with the "Little Apocalypse" in the Gospels of Matthew and Luke, and go from there to certain references in the epistles of Paul and John. Inevitably one is led to the final book in the Bible, Revelation. The Book of Revelation leads the student back to the Book of Daniel, where most of the figures and symbols were borrowed. These, in turn, came from the Chaldean culture.*

Using this method, Russell took on any and all biblical scholars of his day. He announced time and again that all of them were wrong all of the time, and that they had not translated or interpreted correctly. He kept on rummaging around in the scriptural attic for the needed and desired proof texts, using the jigsaw method.

He saw mankind now struggling in the last days in the battle between Satan and Jehovah, the former having ruled the world since the time of Adam, and the latter (Jehovah) trying to get His kingdom back. Russell denied the divinity of Christ and the doctrine of the Trinity, among other accepted Christian doctrines. Unaware that for centuries,

---

*An example of this process of borrowing is the assignment of the four symbols representing the four Evangelists. They are depicted as the face of a man (Matthew), the face of an eagle (John), the face of a lion (Mark), and the face of a bull (Luke). These are the four symbols for the cardinal points of the Babylonian compass, Matthew being north. These figures also represent the fixed astrological signs for air, water, fire, and earth in the zodiac. As one might suspect, there are parallel personalities in the Old Testament. Isaiah shares the spot with Matthew, Daniel with John, Ezekiel with Mark, and Jeremiah with Luke. As if this were not enough, the tribes of Judah are each assigned a spot in the zodiac, as well as the twelve apostles. Combined, they are the "four and twenty elders" from Revelation 4:7-10.

The sources for this information are many and varied, mostly from nineteenth-century biblical scholarship. However, on the floor at the crossing of the Chapel of the Dormition, Mt. Zion, Jerusalem, a zodiac wheel thirty feet in diameter is set in mosaic delineating the above figures. It dates from Crusader days (1150 A.D.). This lore was known by the Crusaders through ancient Masonry, probably including "pyramidism," a subject which fascinated Russell.

eastern and western religionists have alike said that man *is* a living soul and *has* a body, Russell trumpeted this about as though it was news—which it probably was in the world that he had been living in. His growing number of followers also rejoiced in this new insight into the nature of man.

He also asserted that man does not have an immortal soul. His original complaint against the teachings of the mainline churches, as they are frequently called today, was solved to his own satisfaction when he decided that the Hebrew word *Sheol,* which means "the underworld of the dead" or "place of shadows," should be translated "the common grave of mankind." He goes on to say that the word *Sheol* is used sixty-five times in the Old Testament. Three times it is translated "pit," thirty-one times it is translated "grave," and thirty-one times it is translated as "hell." "These are all faulty translations," Russell avers, adding, ". . . if measured by the present general use of the words hell, grave, and pit."

His band of followers increased as more and more persons were banded together in his Bible Study Groups. Russell's explanation that Jesus had invisibly returned in 1874 completely satisfied his inquirers. According to Russell's reckonings the end of the gentile times meant the end of the world as he and his followers knew it. By his computations the date for the beginning of the end was the year 1914. This would mark the transformation of the believers into spirit creatures and associates of Jesus. The intervening thirty years were devoted to the refining of this expectancy through his magazine and other writings.

Many of the Bible Study Groups shepherded and taught by Russell, either in person or through the *Watchtower* magazine, began calling him "pastor," a title he understandably began to use himself. The increasing number of readers and subscribers of his magazine were encouraged in every issue to form groups to study Scripture, using the magazine articles as source materials and following the lessons printed in each issue. Within three years—by 1880—Russell had been chosen as head of nearly thirty groups in Delaware, Massachusetts, Michigan, New Jersey, New York, Ohio, and Pennsylvania. He tried to visit each congregation regularly in person.

The single-mindedness of this gentle, kindly, and obstinate man was remarkable. John Bunyan, who never did find a congenial home in any church in seventeenth-century England, and who was put in jail frequently by church authorities for refusal to attend services of divine worship on the Sabbath, never received any help or understanding from the religious leaders of his day. So, too, was the fate of Charles Taze Russell, except that one can detect a strain of anger in the sensitive and egoistic Russell in his reactions to the treatment he received as compared to the milder reactions of Bunyan.

Known by outsiders at first as "Millennial Dawnists," they soon became known as "Russellites." (This is most marked in England, where the movement took root early. The name "Russellite" stuck and persisted in Britain even after the name "Jehovah's Witnesses" became the official title after the accession of Judge Rutherford, as yet thirty years away.) By whatever name they were known, these people had one communion service a year. Held in Pittsburgh, it was called the Anniversary Supper. Pastor Russell declared that it should be observed on the exact anniversary of the original Last Supper, the fourteenth of Nisan, that is, the first Thursday after the full moon of the spring equinox. This method of figuring from the ancient lunar calendar still is used in western Christendom to determine the date of Easter, and of course, the Witnesses' Anniversary Supper also coincides with the Jewish Passover, the Liturgy of Recall. This annual spring communion also served as a convention and get-together in

Pittsburgh for all Russellites who could possibly arrange their lives so that they could be present for the happy occasion.

The form of church government that Russell introduced was the form with which he previously had been the most familiar, namely that of the nineteenth-century Congregational Church. Each group elected its own board of elders or directors for annual terms. Russell made it clear that he regarded this form of government as the only form that was scripturally approved. He explained that the method of selecting and ordaining elders in the churches is by congregational election. This is followed by the stretching forth of the hands in vote toward the person thus selected.

He always had a most emphatic endorsement of democratic procedures in his ideas of church polity. Many years later his successor, Judge Rutherford, successfully attempted to rid the growing church of this system in favor of the centralized appointment of all congregational officials, thus producing the current method of leadership appointment from the head office.

Pastor Russell urged his people continually to spread the good news by distributing the tracts that began to appear. One of his first books was called *Food for Thinking Christians* (1880). It was heavily promoted through the magazine, as were the increasing numbers of tracts and booklets that he was constantly writing as he continued to develop the theology and doctrine of the society.

In 1884 the organization was chartered as a corporation under the title, "Zion's Watch Tower Tract Society." This was the forerunner of the present Watch Tower Bible and Tract Society of Pennsylvania. This latter remains one of the three legal instruments of the Jehovah's Witnesses.

For nearly twenty years the growth was solid, steady, and rapid. The Bible House was built in Pittsburgh in

1889, a four-story building that had an assembly hall seating over two hundred. There was also a small printing plant, as one might expect by now. There was a shipping room and editorial office. There were living quarters for personnel.

Just prior to this time, Pastor Russell's first full-length book was published; it was entitled *The Divine Plan of the Ages* (1886). In his characteristic fashion he took on any and all adversaries. The thoughts and prevailing opinions of theologians were ignored completely. He paid no attention whatsoever to the writing of the early Church Fathers, if indeed he was even aware of their existence as a body of writings dealing with the Church and belief during the first three hundred years of the Church's life. He damned the Roman Catholic Church and identified the papacy as the anti-Christ. He accused this body, along with the Church of England, the Anglican Communion, and the See of Canterbury of distorting pure doctrine and actively discouraging private and group Bible study. In fairness to Russell, there may have been some truth to this latter charge. At that time, the Reformation was still being fought in the English Church, and it also had its hands full with the attack of the new scientism brought about by the Darwin-Huxley revolution. The Anglican Church was in a state of ferment in that it wasn't sure where it did stand.

Russell dismissed Protestantism as groups of people who have made little progress through the break from history because of their preference for gathering around their favorite leaders instead of walking in the light. The Pastor charged directly into the Darwinian camp:

> Surely, if unintelligent nature were the creator or evolver, she would continue the process, and there would be no such thing as a fixed species, since without intelligence nothing would arrive

> at fixed conditions. Evolution would be a fact to-
> day, and we would see about us fish becoming
> birds and monkeys becoming man . . . .
> —*The Divine Plan of the Ages*

One gleans from the pages of *The Watchtower,* and Russell's tract writings, that Jehovah's great creative week might have been 40,000 years before the appearance of Adam and Eve, more confidently announced as occurring about 6000 B.C.E. Russell regarded the prevailing opinions of the uniformitarian scientists and scholars as indulging in geological guesses of millions of years. This was plain nonsense to Charles Taze Russell.

Without knowing that he was voting for Arius against Athanasius in the Nicene Creed controversy of 325 C.E., he explained that there were two perfect men, Adam and Jesus. The difference being that Adam failed to stay perfect and that Jesus enhanced His perfection:

> When Jesus was in the flesh he was a perfect
> human being; previous to that time he was a
> perfect spiritual being; and since his resurrection
> he is a perfect spiritual being of the highest or
> divine order.
> —*Jehovah's Witness in the Divine Purpose*

This book was the first in what became a series of six called *Studies in the Scriptures.* The original name was "Millennial Dawn," but was soon altered. A seventh volume was written by Russell in his later years and did not come into print until after his death. The total set contained the whole doctrine of the Society until 1920, four years after his death. It is interesting to note that the great bulk of Russell's voluminous writings are seldom, if ever, quoted by modern Witness writers (all are anonymous).

Nor are any of the Pastor's books reprinted by the Society. Indeed, few Witnesses have any familiarity with any of Russell's writings or even with his life story. They are naturally aware of his person in somewhat the same sense as a devout Christian may be of certain saints or patriarchs who left no written record behind them.

The Pastor's literary output has fallen into disuse because the Society has moved on from its earlier position during Russell's heyday. But his memory as the patriarch-founder remains.

It was not until several years after Pastor Russell had departed this life that the taboo on blood transfusions was added to the policy and practice of the Witnesses. Prior to World War I, the use of blood transfusions was minimal. This practice came into general and accepted use in western medicine in the nineteen twenties. During Russell's day it had not yet become an issue on which the Witnesses needed to take a stand.

There is also in these volumes the distinct idea that the end of the world was expected to come about in 1914 or 1915. He wrote that, according to his computations, the month of October in 1914 seemed to be the most likely. However, he never did say flatly that this was the date. He did leave an escape hatch open and admitted the risks of predicting such an event as the millennium:

> It is not to be considered strange if some suggestions made in this volume have not been fulfilled with absolute accuracy to the very letter.
> —*The Time Is at Hand*

In addition, Russell was fascinated with the mystery of the Great Pyramid of Cheops. In his third volume of studies he goes on at great length analyzing the figures and measurements of its interior and exterior. He believed the pyramid to be a "Bible in stone" and "strong corroborative witness to God's plan." To him it was a repository of historic and prophetic truths. He even accepted the belief that God inspired Pharaoh to have it built according to a secret key that, once turned in the lock, would show everything there to be in complete agreement with his own interpretations, even about the millennial year of 1914! Mentioning Pastor Russell's interest in "Pyramidism" does nothing but make the modern-day Witness suspect that you are "putting him on."

As the movement continued to grow and prosper, Pastor Russell himself became something of a spellbinding speaker. He spoke six to eight hours a day either in small group instructions or assembly hall crowds. Much of his time was spent directing and administering the Society from a railroad coach. He was constantly on the move going back and forth across the continent, always challenging the local clergy to debate with him. He did his utmost to visit as many local congregations as he possibly could. It was a growing custom to elect him a sort of pastor-in-absentia.

While he was warmly received by his followers wherever he traveled, his returns to his home had become something of an ordeal. He was living, as he knew that many of his followers likewise were, in a "matrimonial furnace of affliction." Russell had married in 1879. His wife had shared the work, including the editorial chores involved in publishing *The Watchtower*. After eighteen years of a childless marriage, she began to disagree with her husband over the way the magazine was to be run. Finally, in 1897, she separated from him. After six years she filed suit for a legal separation. Even in those days it took three years for a case to reach the courts.

One of her many complaints had to do with an orphan girl the Russells had taken into their home. When questioned on this subject, Russell made one of the most unfortunate public statements of his entire life. He replied, "I am like a jellyfish. I float here and there. I touch this one and that, and if she responds I take her to me, and if not, I float on to others." That statement almost proved his total undoing. He was nicknamed "The Jellyfish Pastor" by the press. That would have been the *coup de grâce* to almost any public figure, but not to Russell.

Another five years passed with continual disputes over alimony figures. Finally he was forced to come up with $9,-000 to settle the matter. His followers provided the amount. However, literally thousands of disenchanted students left the ranks after this sensational trial and court action.

Russell's troubles were far from over. They were actually just beginning for him. The organization had begun selling a product called "Miracle Wheat." It was sold for a dollar a pound or $60.00 a bushel. A quintuple yield was promised. A few tests here and there revealed that Miracle Wheat was like any other wheat, having no special traits or qualities. Russell's defense was that the scheme was not much different from church bakery sales. He stated that he had tasted some rather inferior pies from such sales that were sold at high prices and promises, too, but that they were done for the good of the Order.

A Brooklyn paper printed a cartoon satirizing Miracle Wheat. Russell filed suit for libel. He not only lost, but was required to refund the money to the wheat buyers. Shortly afterwards he was into another business. This time he promoted a cure for cancer. However, it was the third "cave-in" that nearly destroyed all his work.

As we know, he was forever challenging clergy to debate. He was also accusing *all* biblical scholars of making one mistake after another in their scriptural inquiries and studies. He filled his books and the magazine with discussions of the correct meaning of the different Greek and Hebrew words. He had come to regard himself not only as the outstanding biblical scholar—which he was not—but attempted with some success for a while to pose as an educated expert and professional in the field of Biblical Criticism. This was never doubted by his followers—and never accepted by others.

This debacle was also his own doing. He had received a copy of a pamphlet from Canada in which he was accused of being a false scholar:

> This person never attended the higher schools of learning. He knows comparatively nothing of philosophy, systematic or historical theology, and is totally ignorant of the dead languages.

His accuser was a Baptist minister from Hamilton, Ontario. Pastor Russell was put on the stand in the police court in Hamilton in 1913, and that proved to be his undoing. He was asked if he knew the Greek alphabet. He answered that he did. He was then pressed to state whether or not he could tell the individual Greek letters when he saw them, to which Russell admitted that he might make a mistake in identifying some of them. There was some stalling and dodging, then finally the direct question: "Are you familiar with the Greek language?" Trapped, he had to admit that he was not. He was further maneuvered into admitting that he did not know Latin or Hebrew, either. That was that. The Pastor lost the case.

Early in his work he had come across what is known as the *Interlinear Translation of the New Testament*. This work, by British scholars Westcott and Hort, presented the Greek text. Underneath each word the corresponding English word appeared in every case where it was at all possible. This book has been a staple of every student of the New Testament in all seminaries since the early 1880s, and Russell became remarkably adept at word-matching, and among his followers—who knew nothing of this field of study—there was only admiration for Russell's learning.

Through this approach, and having no knowledge whatsoever of linguistics, he asserted that each word, Greek, Latin, or Hebrew, had but *one* meaning. It was quite beyond him to grasp the subtleties of language whereby the same word means different things in different contexts. Russell would have none of it. The word *stauros,* meaning "a cross" or "a stake," is an example. To Russell and his successors it could not mean both. It *had* to be one or the other.

Shortly after this succession of misfortunes—especially the divorce—the work was moved to Brooklyn. Russell managed to purchase the former home of Henry Ward Beecher, the minister of the Plymouth Congregational Church. He also bought a small church nearby that had been known as "Plymouth Bethel." Some name trading took place now. The Beecher home was renamed "Bethel," and the church was called the Brooklyn Tabernacle. From here the work began to reach out more and more. The Pastor began a syndicated weekly column, printing weekly sermons for newspapers around the country to subscribe to. At one time there were over 1,500 newspapers subscribing to the service. It was suddenly abandoned in 1915, the year before Russell's death. By this time the sales of his books were in the millions. *The Watchtower* prospered also.

One of the most remarkable of Russell's latter-day feats was the production called the "Photo-drama of Creation." He had the vision and foresight to see that moving picture spectaculars were coming in the foreseeable future. Immediately he saw its possibility as a method of extending and promoting his millennial convictions. In the early days of experiment and production, Russell was in the midst of it.

Using a combination of slides, film, and phonograph records, he produced the first of the visual aid techniques. This first venture cost the Society over $300,000, a fantastically high price even for those days. To give one an idea of the immensity of the scope of the project: the complete showing took eight hours (mercifully divided into two four-hour sections). Several sets of this presentation were made and distributed throughout the United States, Canada, and England. It has been estimated that as many as 35,000 people saw this show daily when it was at its height. The total audience has been conservatively estimated to be a figure in excess of 9,000,000 persons.

Meanwhile, Armageddon is coming up. A heedless world went right on with its wicked ways, unaware that the coming January 1, 1914, ushered in the fateful year of the end of the Gentile times. Nobody but Russell's followers believed that this was to be Jehovah's year of decision, that the nations would be overthrown, and that the new Eden was about to burst forth upon a tired and weary world. The old-timers waited with confident expectancy for that day—some of them had waited for over thirty years. These were the ones who knew beyond all doubt that they were of the remnant, numbered among the 144,000 that would rule in heaven for a thousand years with King Jesus. They believed completely that sometime during that year they would join Jesus Christ in the spirit-life in heaven, assisting in the management and administration of creation. This was a true elite, for not even the great men of the Old Testament were included, for they had been born before the new dispensation. The more recent converts could thank God that they heard the news in time. They knew that they were not likely to be among the 144,000, but at least they would receive an eternal life on a pain-free earth, free at last from suffering.

The weeks and months rolled by and nothing much happened, except a marked increase in the anxiety load that Pastor Russell was carrying. Toward the end of the year he wrote:

> Even if the time of our change should not come within ten years, what more should we ask? Are we not a blessed, happy people? Is not our God faithful? If any of you find anything better, let him take it. If any of you ever find anything better, we hope you will tell us.

The year closed with no word from Jehovah God. Charles Taze Russell increased by one more the long line of mistaken prophets whose doomsday came and went without event.

Although the Society did not evaporate or go to pieces, it was some years later before an acceptable explanation emerged—from Pastor Russell's successor. Russell himself had two more years to live. The explanation that was eventually forthcoming was that the year 1914 was the start of the tremendous battle in heaven between Satan and Jesus (who actually was Michael the Archangel reincarnated on earth). Jesus had won very quickly. Satan was thrown down upon earth and restricted there, as far as his activities were concerned. Now, having to confine his evil doings to a planet that he was making miserable during the short time remaining to him, he started a war, a famine, and the breakdown in morals that followed.

Presumably this is the same situation today, except that the end *does* seem nearer. All signs point to humanity coming apart at the seams, with the decline and deterioration of the nation-state, corruption of government, and the dissipation and deterioration of the family as a social unit.

In the fall of 1916 Pastor Russell began what turned out to be his final nationwide barnstorming tour. He made it to Los Angeles, California, where, due to his increasing weakness, he was required to address the assemblies seated in a chair. At this point he decided to cancel his exhausting tour and begin the ride home. He died in his private Pullman coach while parked on a siding in Pampa, Texas. His final request was, "Make me a Roman toga." His dutiful aide did the best he could with two Pullman sheets. He wrapped the Pastor up in them, called the conductor and porter and announced, "We want you to see how a great man of God can die."

Charles Taze Russell, every inch the white-bearded patriarch, with dignity gathered the sheet around him while sitting on the edge of the bed. In the manner in which the passing of Jacob is described in the Bible, so too did Pastor Russell draw up his feet, turn on his side with a sigh, and was gathered to his fathers at the earthly age of sixty-four, still looking and hoping for the great day of Jehovah God.

4

"Theocracy Ever Increasing"— the Administration of Judge Rutherford

Whatever one may say or think about the leadership of the Jehovah's Witnesses since the time of Pastor Russell to this day, one must acknowledge their competency and talents. It was no small task on the part of Charles Taze Russell to take as unpromising a group on as uncertain and shaky ground as those millennial visions of his and to mold a society out of it. But this he did, in spite of the defeats that he experienced at the hands of his wife, the courts, and the press.

The work of his successor was likewise impressive, and yet in quite a different and remarkable way. So too, was the second successor in due time. The Witnesses have certainly been blessed with a trinity of contrasting and gifted leaders throughout their history of a hundred years. Individually, each one of these three leaders survived a number of personal Armageddons—to their individual credit.

The Society somehow survived a very shaky period following the death of their founding leader, the patriarchal Pastor. Many of them began to think that they would soon be following their beloved leader into the eternal kingdom. They believed that with his death the missionary work was now completed, and the world had been warned. Why else, many of them reasoned, would the Lord call their leader at the comparatively young age of sixty-four? Some thought that the kingdom could not possibly be more than ten years off at the most. This would have brought Russell's age to seventy-five—certainly a more appropriate age for a patriarch to be gathered to his fathers. *The Watchtower* explained that apparently there was other work to be accomplished first, and that possibly Pastor Russell was on "the other side" speeding up the day of judgment when "the secrets of all hearts shall be disclosed."

One of the few professional men to join the Society was a lawyer named Joseph F. Rutherford. He was baptized and received into the movement as a full-time pilgrim within a year—by the time he was thirty-eight years old. He had grown up as a member of a most strict Baptist family distinguished for austerity and having a strong touch of conservative rural Missouri flavor. His father, a true midwestern anti-intellectual, finally consented to have his son attend an academy. The understanding was, however, that his son hire a substitute to take over his own farm chores. One has to admire Joseph Rutherford for his survival quotient and his persistency against such frustrating odds. Stay with it he did, though, and he proceeded to procure an education for himself. By the time he was twenty-two years of age, he became a lawyer and began practice in Booneville, Missouri. It is on record that on various occasions when the regular judge became ill or unavoidably absent, then Rutherford took his turn with the other lawyers as a stand-in. Here, then, is where he acquired the title "Judge," although he was never elected to that office, and did not likely substitute for the incumbent on more than four or five occasions. To be fair about it, he never referred to himself by this title. It was his personal followers and publicity men who established the custom and began addressing him in person and print as Judge Rutherford.

The story is that two Witness missionary ladies, out on their rounds, called on Rutherford in his law office. He was about twenty-five years old at the time. He listened to them, buying three books written by Pastor Russell. More than twelve years passed before he took any direct action toward joining the Society. It came about that sometime in 1900 he met Pastor Russell on one of the prophet's missionary journeys. Russell urged him to write down his religious views. Rutherford did just that, and came up with a book called *Man's Salvation from a Lawyer's Point of View*. By this time he had been practicing law for sixteen years. Now, having finally received the baptism, Rutherford almost immediately took over the legal work of the Society for Pastor Russell.

In appearances this man Rutherford, all six feet, four inches of him, looked more like a judge than any judge that anybody could remember, and then some. Autocratic, austere, positive and opinionated, he wore a wing collar and a black bow tie at all times. He carried either a cane or an umbrella on his arm. His reading glasses hung from a black ribbon to complete the picture of sobriety, dignity, and judgeship. He was brusque and direct in his dealings, a bit formidable perhaps, especially when compared to the gentle, easygoing, kindly, and gregarious Charles Taze Russell, the lovable prophet.

Although he was almost the direct opposite in temperament from Russell, he succeeded the Pastor with a unanimous vote in January of 1917. He set out right away to remake *The Watchtower* into his own image and likeness. Naturally, after the departure of Pastor Russell into the larger life in the eternal realms there was a lingering admiration and worship for the Pastor. Rutherford was faced with that same old problem that afflicts every pastor who is the successor to a beloved minister who has served for many years in the same parish. In each and every one of these cases, the successor learns at once that many changes are demanded immediately, and yet he must move carefully. Many things tend to deteriorate and disintegrate when the elder leader holds things together somehow in his later years through sheer will power, overcoming weariness and fatigue. This was precisely what Rutherford discovered on his first day in office. It was "Pastor Russell always did it this way," or "This isn't the way he had us do it." The Judge knew ahead of time, though, that many devotees had regarded Russell as the wise and faithful servant mentioned by Jesus in Matthew 24:45. During his latter years the cagey old Pastor let it ride that way, neither correcting nor denying the accolade. The Judge (as he was immediately called) explained that "servant" referred to the Watchtower Society and not to any particular individual.

Before Judge Rutherford came into full and complete control of the Society, there were some shaky times for him. He had yet to survive a power struggle. This was triggered from an unsuspected source, the leader of the Society in England. This man, P. S. L. Johnson, had been a Jewish Lutheran minister who had gone onward into the light of English Russellism. Succumbing to the temptation to take over the Society in England on Pastor Russell's death, he made his play, and the word soon hit the home office. Rutherford ordered him to return to Brooklyn and give a steward's account of the work there. Murmuring and grumbling, he returned. He politicked with the members of the Board of Directors. He managed to persuade four of them to oppose the new leadership.

The Judge was more than equal to the trial by fire. His years spent in practicing Missouri law were not in vain. The meeting of the Society scheduled for Boston was coming up. Rutherford, serving as permanent chairman, never recognized members of the opposition when they sought their turns on the floor of the convention. In that way he controlled every session. He next pulled a rare legal maneuver. This was based on Pastor Russell's casual custom of filling positions on the various boards by his personal appointment without confirmation, although the process technically or canonically required it. Even though it was required by their constitution and by-laws, still nobody had ever dared to take issue with Pastor Russell to his face, especially in public meeting. Rutherford knew that every one of his enemies had been appointed by Russell without the confirmation of the Society. Rutherford peremptorily declared them out of office because they did not legally hold their positions on the various boards. The dissenters were thus quickly removed and replaced by the Judge with men who were then and there approved by convention.

The upshot of this maneuver was the loss of about 4,000 members, leaving a loyal remnant of nearly 17,000 of the faithful. Some of these dropouts formed splinter groups. The largest of these dissident groups tried to continue primitive and original Russellism, calling themselves the "Dawn Bible Students Association."

They turned out to be a hardy Isaianic remnant. From time to time during Rutherford's reign, congregations would occasionally be split into opposing factions as he molded the Society into a new form, thus gradually removing "pure" Russellism. These "Dawnites" later produced television programs. They publish a magazine called *The*

Dawn. They continue to distribute Pastor Russell's original *Studies in Scriptures.* While they deny the divinity of Christ and the existence of hell—as the Pastor did—they do not follow the Witnesses in their hostility toward other Christian bodies. They present their teachings to all who will listen. They do so quietly, assuring themselves that the rejecters at least received one more chance to embrace the truth before the Day of Wrath.

The Dawnites teach that all men, both good and evil, will be given a second chance. This includes Adam, too. This is a point that the Witnesses could not meet. Also, as with Pastor Russell, who had nothing to say against blood transfusions, the Dawnites see nothing basically wrong with them. One should bear in mind, however, that in Russell's day transfusion was not yet a common practice, certainly not to the degree that might have required a scriptural opinion from him.

The Servants of Yah were another tine off the old pitchfork. They claimed to have arrived at a special esoteric knowledge of the Bible by reading the original Hebrew text and ignoring the vowel point system. By way of some rather obscure reasoning they developed their own system and then claimed that only 144,000 persons were ever expected or even destined to understand the hidden meaning of Scripture and be able to glean any sense from it. And so they go, but so did Judge Rutherford and the Society. But here follows a period in the history of the Society in which one cannot help but admire the members of the Society for their faithfulness and tenacity—which makes one wonder whether the twentieth-century Christian could stand up to defending his culture-religion.

Rutherford soon came out with a book entitled *The Finished Mystery* (1918). Within a year's time more than three quarters of a million copies had been printed and sold. The book was an attack against *all* organized religions. Catholics and Protestants alike were tarred from the same barrel and identified as "modern day Babylon." The violence and energy of this book brought the Society to the attention of the Canadian government immediately. It banned the Society from functioning in the country. The ensuing conflict centered on the issue of refusing military service. This eventually brought them into conflict with the United States Government as soon as America became embroiled in the first World War.

Stories started around that German officials had visited the Brooklyn offices of the Society just before Congress declared war on Germany. Their offices were raided. Eight Watchtower officials were arrested for sedition. It was claimed that they had violated the Espionage Act because they obstructed recruitment to the armed forces of the nation and encouraged insubordination. Seven of these eight defendants, including their leader, Judge Rutherford, received twenty years on each of four counts, to run concurrently. The eighth defendant got off with a ten-year sentence.

When the verdict was announced, the Bible students in court began to sing "Blessed Be the Tie that Binds" as the defendants were led away to begin their sentences. Judge Rutherford, ever equal to a crisis, announced that this was the happiest day of his life because he was now able to serve earthly punishment for the sake of his belief. "It is indeed a great privilege," he concluded.

Less than 4,000 followers remained faithful as the war fever mounted in the land. Throughout the nation the Society's Bible students were being dragged through the streets. These people became true martyrs as their successors would be in Germany in World War II.

While in prison the Judge wrote a weekly letter to those on the outside who remained faithful. He and his colleagues organized Bible classes among the inmates in the Federal Prison in Atlanta. But evil days had fallen upon the Society. The Tabernacle was sold. Bethel House was closed and the office moved back to Pittsburgh. Through all the adversity the Society somehow kept going.

Within six months over 700,000 signatures had been obtained. The Watchtower officials were released on $10,000 bail while awaiting a new trial. The court declared that the defendants did not receive the impartial trial to which they were entitled. The decision was reversed. A case of true irony comes to the surface not too many years later. Judge Rutherford himself argued before the Supreme Court of the United States in the first of many legal tests on the rights of Witnesses.

One can understand how this unjust prison experience and this rather spectacular miscarriage of justice shaped the Society's emerging idea of itself as a separate nation of Jehovah's people. It is from these roots that the idea of a theocracy grew. The Judge's heart had been hardened in the days of provocation toward both the nation and its churches, for both had teamed up against the Society during the heat and fever of the early days of World War I.

It was truly a start from scratch when the released leaders tried to gather up the fragments of a Society. The real estate had been sold. The workers who had lived in Bethel had gone their separate ways. The presses were gone. There was nothing. Moreover, their leader was ill from his prison stay—a condition from which he never completely recovered. He went to California to convalesce from his respiratory thorn in the flesh. Admirably, what Bible students there were who remained managed to continue putting out regular issues of *The Watchtower*. Within three years the Society emerged from its own ashes at a convention in 1922. They were three thousand strong and on the road to rapid recovery.

This was truly a new start in every way. First of all came

the remodelling and reshaping of doctrine. It was maintained that up to the present time there had been a misplaced emphasis on character development, for one thing, and there had been an idolatrous attitude toward the founder, the now-sainted Charles Taze Russell, whose ghost was still in Rutherford's closet. Moreover, it was declared that the celebration of Christmas was to be done away with at once because it had been inherited from earlier pagan traditions. The use of the cross was forbidden as a symbol of faith. It was now explained that Jesus Christ did not die upon a cross but upon an upright torture stake. Rutherford also maintained that the Society, up until the present, had not given proper honor to the name Jehovah God, and that this was going to be observed from now on. These changes happily did not happen all at once, even though the history of the Society would lead one to think so. The cross continued to be used in book illustrations. The name of Jehovah appeared gradually more and more, not suddenly.

One interesting aspect of Pastor Russell's thought and practice was his use of involved calculations based on the symbolism and the mathematics of the Great Pyramid of Cheops in Egypt. He had used these ancient figures to support his own chronology of the Old Testament. Rutherford continued this aid for a brief period but finally threw the whole idea out, maintaining that only the Bible itself was a trustworthy guide to prophecy. Pastor Russell had also been fascinated with all kinds of charts. Some were borrowed. Some were developed by himself. He had spread them here and there throughout his writings to assist in the study of Scripture. Out went the charts. Russell was gradually disappearing in the distance.

The precipitating cause for abandoning such techniques might well have been the Judge's prediction that Abraham, Jacob, Isaac, David, and other patriarchs would appear on earth in 1925. Because they had been born too early, they were not eligible to be among the 144,000, but would assist with the earthly rule after Armageddon. The appearance of these dignitaries would mark the beginning of the guns of Armageddon and the final battle against Satan and his forces. Rutherford even bought a beautiful home for them in San Diego, California. They would be provided for during the days of provocation on the assumption that they had already had their crises. When none of the patriarchs showed up to live in the land of the palm, the olive, and the star pine, no further mention of it was made. Within five years Judge Rutherford moved into the house himself. He remained there until his death in 1942.

The Society was directed from Abraham's study even though the administration and publishing were done with renewed vigor at the old site of Bethel in Brooklyn.

The exile of 1918 in Atlanta prison became ancient history as the years went by. The memory of the Beloved Pastor grew faint and dim. Many of the old-timers had long since defected and become Dawnists or had joined other millennial hope groups, or in sheer discouragement gave up trying to believe that the puzzle could ever be solved. By 1930 very few of the Bible students had ever known Pastor Russell. He was little more than a name to them.

With wisdom and foresight Judge Rutherford not only visited the Society in England and reviewed the work there, but he went on to Egypt and the Holy Land in 1920. As a result his writings on Scripture became first-hand, real, vivid, and personal. This experience has saved the lives of many clergymen who had been homiletically dry for years. It has brought new life and understanding into their own preaching and teaching, thus serving as a job-saver. Rutherford's pilgrimage was a dramatic and effective shot in the arm to the movement.

Shortly after the Judge's return, modern printing equipment was purchased. He set about at once to expand *The Watchtower* and *The Golden Age* (later known as *Awake!*). New tracts were appearing one after another. Rutherford urged his followers, "Advertise! Advertise! Advertise!" He began to increase the shrunken membership list. He worked his way through the wreckage of the near-breakup of the Society by World War I and the aftermath of the failure of the Second Coming to materialize. The Judge was turning out to be a more prolific writer than Russell had been. During his twenty-five year tenure, he produced over a hundred books and pamphlets reaching a combined circulation of a third of a billion copies. The Society seemed to be more of a publishing house than a religious organization.

There was another change of strategy coming up. The volunteer door-to-door salesmen were instructed to sell Rutherford's first book, *The Harp of God*. The Society also began asking for donations toward the cost of the tracts and books. Pastor Russell's seven volumes were finally given up and allowed to go out of print while the Judge's writings appeared in profusion. Following closely upon the publication and sale of *The Harp of God* there appeared four more books. Over a million copies of these were printed and offered for sale on the market at prices much below the price of mass-market books.

His insistent urging to advertise had a response throughout the Society, beginning with the home office. The Judge came up with a title and a slogan that is still in effective use today: "Millions Now Living Will Never Die!" This was naturally intended to arouse a person's curiosity and self-interest. What Rutherford actually meant was that humanity was on its last lap around Satan's racetrack, and that only a favored few would make it down the stretch and to the finish line.

Rutherford's impressive aggressive and hostile nature produced enough energy to oppose politics, big business, and organized religion on all fronts at all times. In print, he called the clergy lepers. Anybody who opposed *The Watchtower* opposed the Judge and was thereby a despiser of those who strove to do good. "They may outwardly have a show of godliness," he noted, "but they have no [spiritual] power." His followers were encouraged to picket Roman Catholic churches on Sunday mornings with signs reading, "Religion is a Snare and a Racket." Not surprisingly, the pickets were roughed up on such occasions by indignant churchmen.

In 1925, the Judge came through with a new revelation that Satan had been confined to earth since being cast out of heaven in 1914. This accounted for the calamities of the twenties such as the "Babylonish behavior of the people" and the union of politics and big business. It was at this time that the faithful were assured that when Armageddon began, the faithful would be allowed to stand aside. They would not be required to take part in the slaughter because of their pacifist convictions. On the contrary, they were assured of grandstand seats at the spectacle.

When there was a leveling off in the increase of members and converts—making the future seem less than bright—the quick moving and resourceful Rutherford adopted new methods of evangelism. The Society pioneered in radio evangelism. They began with their own station, WBBR on Staten Island, the Borough of Richmond. For a brief period they also operated WORD in Batavia, Illinois, as well as a small number of stations here and there around the nation. A variation on Russell's newspaper syndicated Bible lessons was also experimented with. Then he had a new strategy that was truly unique. The Judge recorded several sermons on phonograph records that were provided to radio stations around the country. Out of this venture grew the idea and practice of having door-to-door representatives of the Society carry portable phonographs on their rounds and play the Judge's records for any and all householders who became trapped in their own doorways.

The spiral of upward growth began again. A new building was erected on the site of the Beecher home in 1926. Now there was a nine-story office building and residence to house the increasing full-time staff which was needed to handle the tremendous increase in the volume of work to be turned out.

But the greatest stroke of genius by this man was the settling once and for all on the official name of the Society. For years they had been known variously as Bible Students, Millennial Dawnists, Russellites, Watchtower People, and Rutherfordites. The Judge announced to the annual convention in 1931 that he had decided on a proper and fitting name for the Society. He announced that henceforth they would be known as "Jehovah's Witnesses." His text and inspiration came from the Book of the Prophet Isaiah:

> "You are my witnesses," is the utterance of Jehovah . . . .
>
> —Isaiah 43:10, NWT

An added advantage was that all references to the ideas of "witness" and "witnessing" in the Old and New Testaments could be interpreted to mean "Jehovah's Witnesses" specifically. Now it became easy to understand how Abel became the first Witness of Jehovah.

The 1931 convention settled matters internally, but Rutherford still had to challenge religious leaders, especially the Pope, to public debate. The aggressiveness was contagious. The Witnesses began carrying signs—among the first of a picketing generation for the various causes—and thereby found themselves with new ways to become martyred. They stood trial for selling books without a license. They were arrested for disturbing the peace and inciting to riot. It was noted that these were the same charges that were leveled against the first-century Christian witnesses. Then too, they were reminded by the Old Testament, as well as by Jesus, that even the prophets were stoned. The Society's legal department had a full plate of legal business to digest, for they not only defended any and all against whom charges had been made but they further instructed the people how to behave when arrested, how to reach one of the Society's lawyers, and how to stand trial. The Judge was truly in his element, fighting for law and order in the courtroom and in the world.

At the first sign of trouble, the Witness was instructed to contact the Brooklyn office immediately. Call-committees had been arranged to handle these situations. The Society even had a system worked out whereby car caravans could be told to meet at a certain place and descend in a modest horde upon the offending community or neighborhood. While out on such a mission of justice, they would swoop through the area and call upon every householder in the space of two hours or less. The opposition always found himself overmatched in these situations. If the local police began to arrest members of the swarm that had descended, then the jails were quickly filled up and everybody was reached with the news of a coming encounter that would make this teapot tempest look silly. The local mail, being easily filled in most cases, still left many of the Witnesses free to complete their calls unmolested while the Society's lawyers went about the business of springing their colleagues. They won the day—or the night—in each and every case.

The Judge's attacks on religion and the clergy became so vehement that he lost the radio outlets in spite of his attempts to have the FCC intervene. He decided to discontinue broadcasting, except for the few stations they owned. As usual, a frustration was turned into another idea and another victory. The Society bought a fleet of sound trucks to broadcast their messages, especially in the rural communities.

These reverses led the Society into the use of the new portable phonograph. These were provided at cost for the Witnesses by the home office. The value to the Society was inestimable. Now it was possible for the inarticulate and uncertain Witness to bring the Judge himself into the homes of the people the Society was trying to warn of the impending doom. They were able to enter thousands of homes throughout the country through this device. The Judge recorded over eighty separate talks of four minutes each. America could now be fed a Sunday feast of Rutherford homilies every week.

By this time in the life of the Society, the quota of 144,-000 named in the Book of Revelation had been almost filled. Relatively few candidates remained on earth. Pastor Russell could easily presume that all of his followers would be there when the roll was called up yonder. But the Judge, because of the growth in numbers of Witnesses, discovered another caste. There was spirit-life in heaven for the 144,-000. There was everlasting life on earth for the surplus in a recreated and restored Eden. (There was the alternative of annihilation, a poor and unpopular third choice.) Persons, that is, seemingly born out of time could still have a most attractive and tangible reward. Now the task became one of spreading the word to the millions of other sheep who stood a chance of inheriting the Edenic life.

But at this time a new series of misfortunes and tragedies faced the undaunted Society. The new Nazi government included Witnesses on their list of enemies because of their refusal to give obeisance to the Nazi party or to serve in the army. Soon after, the Society was also banned in Italy. Japan followed shortly thereafter. Property was confiscated. The remaining adherents were persecuted. In Germany many of them were victims of torture and death. The blood of the martyrs was the seed of the Church in a way that had not been expected to work for anti-church people, but it did.

As a result of the violent reactions against the Witnesses created by the antagonisms and hostilities of Judge Rutherford and his embattled faithful, the Society moved closer and closer to a position of isolation from the secular and "pagan" world. The Witnesses, not only as local groups in cities and towns throughout the country but throughout the Order, showed a supreme uninterest in the affairs of men, their governments, nations, states, cities, or towns. They paid no more attention to such structures and arrangements than was absolutely necessary as a minimum. After all, this world was Satan's world. They owed Satan nothing; therefore, they did not run for any kind of office. They declined to vote, even as their first leader had counseled. They steadfastly refused to salute the flag. They had as little to do with unions of any kind beyond the necessary membership to become eligible for employment. Clubs and lodges never have Witnesses listed among their memberships.

The Witnesses could not see the point of giving their children college educations because it was a needless and unnecessary outlay of money to invest in a society, since Armageddon was at hand. It would be better, they said, if young adults spent their time warning their colleagues to flee the coming wrath of Jehovah God. For a short time during World War II, the Society discouraged young people from getting married, suggesting instead that they wait until after Armageddon.* Thus was the theocracy born.

In the times of Pastor Russell, neither he nor any other persons of that period showed any special interest in modifying or producing any new or variant forms of government or administration. Russell had more important matters to keep him busy. He simply and naturally borrowed the polity and administration of the church system with which he was most familiar, that of seventeenth-century Congregationalism. But with rapid social change beginning to come about, everything seemed to be crashing down around the house of Jehovah's loyal Witnesses.

Since the beginning of the Society, it had been the practice for each congregation to elect its own elders and to send their names in to headquarters. This creates an extremely loose and inefficient method of getting things done—as churches are finding out today. The best man is not always elected. The Judge consequently wanted to tighten things up a bit so that the local societies would not suffer through lack of adequate leadership through an unfortunate election of a popular old-timer who had little capacity to do the job required. He had to have a leadership in the local congregations that was both aggressive and responsive to the Brooklyn office.

Early in the nineteen-thirties, Rutherford managed to replace this practice, which had reduced so many congregations to a lackadaisical outlook. He instituted what was called a "Service Committee." Within another five years he was thus able to manage the appointments of local officers directly from his office in Brooklyn. The complete changeover from a congregational system of church government to a theocratic control finally emerged.

---

*The Witnesses have never been against marriage just because of the nearness of Armageddon, although from time to time articles in *Awake!* have discouraged the practice. One may naturally raise the question of why they have children. The main reason is that this phenomenon happens from time to time in the best organized families. There is, however, always the theological justification that a child born into a Witness family is almost certain of inheriting eternal life on earth without having to go through death.

As the nations edged toward World War II, under Satan's maneuvering of the nation-states, the tensions and antipathies against the Witnesses again came to the surface. There were increased and renewed attacks made upon them by both the American Legion and Father Coughlin's Christian Front. The Witnesses claimed that the American Legion was behind the attempt to raid their farm and school at South Lansing, New York, on Flag Day in 1940. Hundreds of cars converged on the site. But having been tipped off, the state police and the sheriff's deputies broke up the "attack" by not allowing anyone to leave his car. The estimate by the Witnesses was that there were over 4,000 Legionnaires in this "army" of siege and attack.

As the next convention approached—usually these affairs were looked forward to eagerly, and they were always attended by ever increasing numbers of the faithful as a possible preparation for the last days—Rutherford had some difficulties in procuring a meeting place that would be large enough. The problem was compounded by the reluctance of many municipalities to play host to a group that invited such violent reactions to their presence. It was hard to find a city that would run the risks and expense of riot and bloodshed. The fairgrounds at Columbus, Ohio, were originally arranged for, but the State of Ohio thought better of it, fearing likely disorder from outside interference. Presumably those in charge of such matters had been warned of what might happen in the event the Witnesses did have their convention there. The feeling was running high against the Witnesses everywhere.

Finally they found makeshift arrangements in Detroit. For this happy occasion, the Witnesses produced their own peace enforcers. They stationed guards armed with heavy sticks throughout the meeting grounds. It was also reported that the Judge was anticipating that Father Coughlin and his people would fly over the convention spot and drop a few bombs here and there among the crowd. After all, this *was* Father Coughlin's home territory—he administered a parish at nearby Royal Oak.

By the time of this convention late in 1940, Judge Rutherford himself assumed the mantle of patriarch. It fell upon him as a natural result of his years of service to the Society and his guiding genius—which had made possible the great growth of the Society beyond Pastor Russell's wildest dreams. But now the Judge was in declining health. Never by temperament as gregarious as Pastor Russell, he withdrew from contact with his followers. He eventually became known as a voice on a phonograph record played on Sunday mornings in homes that Witnesses had managed to get themselves invited into.

After the Detroit convention he retired to the San Diego mansion he had purchased for the use of the returning Old Testament prophets. The Judge would now be on hand to greet them upon their arrival. He had lived there intermittently since 1930 in his attempt to improve the state of his health with the respiratory problems that made life so miserable for him in his latter years.

The Judge had previously predicted that the prophets would soon appear to lend their skills and experience to the organization of the New World Society that would be the remnant of the outcome of Armageddon. This estate was known as *Beth Sarim*, "The House of Princes." The deed was made out to Abel, Noah, Abraham, and David. In the meantime, the Judge moved in so that he would have things in order and ready for them.

The Judge never endured disloyalty or criticism from within the Society. He gained his considerable respect through fear, not affection, as Pastor Russell had done so naturally before him. However, the Judge knew how to run an organization, a skill that the Pastor never did master in his gentle and kindly ways. There is one incident that makes it quite clear as to who was in charge at the store.

The legal adviser of the Society, Olin Moyle, objected to the Judge's public scoldings of the faithful at the Bethel dinner table at headquarters. Characteristically, Rutherford "shot down" his opponent and tormentor but did not "do him in."

Gradually the Judge's physical trials became too great. He departed this life on January 8, 1942, dying of carcinoma at Beth Sarim, the home of the prophets, and was gathered to his fathers.

Judge Rutherford was a formidable and highly competent and energetic leader. During his days as director of the course of Jehovah's Witnesses—twenty-five years—he managed among all his activities and responsibilities to write a full-length book each year. By his latter days, more than thirty-six million copies of his pamphlets had been printed and distributed around the world, appearing in many different languages. There are only a few men who can boast of having reached as many persons as he did through his writings.

Unlike Pastor Russell, the Judge did not require a toga to be buried in. His only request was that he be buried at dawn on the day after his death right there on the estate of the prophets. But it was not possible because of county regulations. Eventually his body was buried at Rossville, New York.

The San Diego mansion, Beth Sarim, was eventually sold. The Judge's books were allowed to go out of print even as he had allowed Pastor Russell's books to do before him, and thus the Judge, too, became another shadow against the wall in the history of the Society. But his mark on the Witnesses is indelible. Since his days, they have lived without a country, these Jehovah's Witnesses. Wherever they are, of course, they are *in* one, but never are they *of* a country.

How can one sing the Lord's song in a strange land?

> Hail the Theocracy, ever increasing!
> Wondrous expansion is now taking place.
> Praise to Jehovah is sung without ceasing
> By those who walk in the light of his face!
> —Jehovah's Witness Songbook

5

"Wondrous Expansion"—
the Leadership of
Nathan Homer Knorr

The Society had been guided into birth by a self-taught Bible student and lay preacher, a man of meager education and gentle affection, a man who cared. He was unaware that he was building piece by piece an organization that would be a wonder and a mystery—the almost completely unexplainable Jehovah's Witnesses. This patriarchal figure was succeeded by a Missouri small-town lawyer, a fighter and scrapper, a most difficult and obtuse man to deal with. He did not tilt windmills only, but everything and every person in his path that posed a threat to his aims and plans for the Society, for himself—and for Jehovah God, too, of course.

The person elected to succeed Judge Rutherford was a totally different kind of person in temperament and appearance from either of his predecessors. He was a man of many apparent and already demonstrated gifts of business and administrative ability. He was also a man who got things done. Nathan Homer Knorr started working in the headquarters office the week after he graduated from high school in Allentown, Pennsylvania. That was in June 1923. His family had been a part of the Society during his high school days. It was during this time in his life when his parents separated themselves from the Reformed Church tradition of their ancestry.

His first job in his life was in the shipping room of the printing department. As did the others, he also gave lectures in the greater New York area on the Bible as it related to the teachings of the Society. A loyal, trustworthy, and hard-working disciple, young Knorr quickly gained the attention and confidence of his superiors. It was not long before he became responsible for the coordination of all the printing activities—a serious and heavy responsibility for one of his years. By the time he had worked for the Society for nine years, he was made general manager of the publishing operation. He was not yet twenty-eight years of age.

Within two more years he was made a director of the Watchtower Bible and Tract Society of New York, one of the several original corporations that eventually became the Jehovah's Witnesses. Within another year he also became director and vice-president of the Watch Tower Bible and Tract Society of Pennsylvania as well. By this time, Nathan Knorr, as anybody in his position would, acknowledged that he was quietly certain that he was numbered among the 144,000 of the remnant of Revelation who would reign in heaven one day with King Jesus Christ.

When the board members of both the Pennsylvania and New York corporations met to elect a successor to Judge Rutherford, the bitterness that characterized the succession of the Judge to Russell's throne was missing. There was no resistance or opposition to Knorr's election. This marked the emergence of Jehovah's Witnesses as a

modern, full-fledged twentieth-century business corporation. It had gradually assimilated the protective coloration
of the big business environment. The days of rugged, in-
dividualistic leadership were over now. With their passing,
there also went the color and charisma that accompanies
zeal, enthusiasm, and the strong sense of destiny and purpose. This observation is not intended to imply that any
momentum was lost; nor does it mean that their raison
d'être was no longer at the heart of what had become big
business. Times had changed, that was all.

Knorr immediately set about to bring the Society into
these latter days of the twentieth century possessed with
more faith, power, and influence than they had ever known
before. The new leader showed right away that he knew
what he was doing. In his incumbency, the membership of
Jehovah's Witnesses has shown an increase of over 700%!
What is the more remarkable is that this has been accomplished during a time when mainline churches,
trumpeting a revival in religious interest, showed a growth
factor that reached sometimes as high as three and four
percent. Even this percentage is suspect when one considers the temptations in the parish office of local congregations to retain many names because of the rather wan
hope that those persons may become reactivated.

Under Judge Rutherford the Witnesses had earned a
reputation for orneriness. Their aggressive foot-in-the-door
tactics and their expressed scorn of all who refused to heed
their warnings certainly placed them far down the list of
needed people in a community or neighborhood. The in-
sulting of potential supporters had to be stopped. The first
thing that this thirty-seven-year-old talented ad-
ministrator and executive in big business did was to begin
an entirely new public relations strategy and structure.

Among the first things to go to make room for the new
offensive were the phonographs and records of the Judge's

abrasive, steamroller sermons. Knorr had probably realized for a long time, but was not in a position to say so, that the Society could never grow through the persistent and insensitive practice of playing Rutherford's records on hostile doorsteps. The time was past when the Society could cover up the educational lacks of the people and their inability to articulate the faith by using the Judge's cement-mixer voice to establish a beachhead for them. He was the first to realize that the day was here when every Witness was going to have to learn how to speak for himself and the Society.

Knorr developed a carefully planned step-by-step program that changed the old ways of working. He realized that each and every Witness was going to have to learn how to deliver short presentations on his or her own, and that each one must be taught how to do so with confidence and no display of aggressiveness, hostility, or other poor manners. Producing fluency, good manners, and an attractive self-confidence was a large order. Knorr not only knew how to do this, but he actually accomplished it in such a way that he was sensationally successful in a short time. And it was all done in his quiet, firm, and executive manner.

In 1942, the Society first presented an inclusive program of adult education designed to mold the Witnesses into confidently assured and friendly door-to-door salesmen for the latter-day last-chance religion. The Society developed a weekly theocratic ministry school to accomplish this goal. No one was to go to the front lines of the struggle against the world without being properly armed. There would be no sheep sent forth among the wolves until they were smart enough to know what to do when they were out in Satan's world. They were provided with the twentieth-century weapon of good public relations. They now had their own self-improvement courses designed to turn them into reasonably polished speakers. No longer was the chin-out hard sell the proper stance for the convinced Witness who claimed inside information on the state of the world and its temporary hold on things. Knorr developed the "soft save" to replace the "hard sell."

During the weeks and months that followed this remodeling job on everybody in the Society, they all underwent a short, intensive course in selling, including instruction in the presentation of both the subject and the person. The followers rapidly became skilled in their new ways of spreading their Gospel. When it was decided late in 1942 that the Society was ready, the word went out from headquarters that every local congregation was to sponsor regular public meetings. They were expected and required to distribute handbills on the Main Street of every city and town in the country. These flyers invited everybody to go to a one-hour program in the local Kingdom Hall on a Sunday afternoon. A series of eight public talks were given out to the local congregations which simply outlined the material to be covered. Shrewdly, it was made quite clear, in print, that there would not be any passing of a collection plate.

An example of how the Society's leadership was emerging into the pattern of a business and corporation personality: the policy was adopted that all future publications of the Society would be published anonymously. No by-lines on *any* printed material were to go out under the sponsorship of the Jehovah's Witnesses. This move cut off at the grass roots any possibility of the growth of a personality cult. It also reduced the possibility of any applecart upsetting by appeal to the total membership in any way. From this point on, nobody but Knorr and the top officers of the corporations knows exactly who writes the books, tracts, and magazine articles. Even the correspondence was simply rubber-stamped, "Watchtower Bible and Tract Society."

The next step in the expansion of the Society was the establishment of the Watchtower Bible School of Gilead. This was located at South Lansing, New York, in the Finger Lake area near Ithaca. This was created to train full-time missionaries who would go wherever they were sent to establish new work. Men and women were sent out all over the world. To them goes the credit for much of the rapid growth enjoyed by the Jehovah's Witnesses during the years of Knorr's leadership. Also, the Witness became known within the Society as a "publisher." This was meant in the original sense of the word *publish*: to announce, to broadcast, to make known.

The new President, through the appointment and commissioning of some veteran Witnesses—several of them college graduates—authorized and undertook a new translation of the Bible.* The so-called faulty translations of Scripture have always frustrated the members of this impatient cult. To them, the words in the older translations did not convey the meaning that they were supposed to. This new commission was to correct that. The New Testament version appeared first, in 1950, and was known as the *New World Translation of the Christian Greek Scriptures.* By 1960, the Old Testament had been completely translated. The words "Old Testament" and "New Testament" are not used by the Witnesses. They prefer to call them the "Hebrew Scriptures" and the "Greek Christian Scriptures," respectively.

The *New World Translation* conforms generally to the older English versions. However, opportunities were taken to insert the word "Jehovah," which the Witnesses consider the proper name of God. The traditional versions more frequently use the word "God" or "Lord." The New World translators also changed "cross" to "torture stake."

---

*Work on the New Testament was begun in 1945 and completed in 1950. The Old Testament translation was completed in 1960.

They also attempted to make clear those passages dealing with Sheol and the immortality of the soul.

The *New World Translation* of the Lord's Prayer indicates how they approach the problems that are always inherent in translating. In this case, they did make the phrases more congenial to their beliefs:

> Our Father in the heavens, let your name be sanctified. Let your kingdom come. Let your will take place, as in heaven, also upon earth. Give us today our bread for this day; and forgive us our debts, as we also have forgiven our debtors. And do not bring us into temptation, but deliver us from the wicked one.
>
> —Matthew 6:9-13, NWT

What is commonly known as the "ascription" ("for thine is the kingdom and the power and the glory") is omitted from this version. Scholars generally agree that it was not part of the original prayer, but was added as a response.

The persistent use of the word "Jehovah" in place of the more accurate "Yahweh" is not the result of ignorance. It is common knowledge that the Hebrews did not write or speak the divine name, but used a group of four letters called the "tetragrammaton." These letters spelled out "YHWH," which, with vowels inserted, came out "Yahweh." The Hebrews substituted their word for "Lord," which is "Adonai." Later Christians took the vowels from "Adonai" and put them between the consonants of "YHWH," thus coming up with Jehovah. Even the New World translators agree that the pronunciation of the divine name was probably closer to "Yahweh" than to "Jehovah," but the Witnesses say:

> While inclining to view the pronunciation "Yahweh" as the more correct way, we have retained

the form "Jehovah" because of the people's familiarity with it since the 14th century. Moreover, it preserves equally with other forms, the four letters of the tetragrammaton JHWH.

The *New World Translation* does not include the Apocrypha, fourteen books not included in the Old Testament, although they were written before the Christian beginnings. The reason for their exclusion was that they were not written in Hebrew, but in Greek. Since the time of Alexander the Great's attempt in the third century B.C.E. to mold all cultures into one culture, and many languages into one language, it had not been permitted to use the Hebrew language in writing literature because its use would be restricted. The Jews argued that this was exactly the point. Unless Scripture was written in God's language (Hebrew), then it cannot well appear among the books that He wrote (or inspired), using the hand of man. Martin Luther gathered these writings together and inserted them between the Old and New Testaments. (They were not included in the King James translation into English) but are available in some of the newer translations of the Bible, that are current today.

In their *New World Translation*, the committee responsible for the work returned to the original Greek text of the New Testament (from which almost all modern translations have been made). They stuck quite closely to a literal translation. In the way that is so characteristic of the Society, dating from Pastor Russell's practice, they stuck to the principle that every word has but a single meaning regardless of context, and that shades of meaning are not possible. A word means what it means what it means.

From the ivy-walled towers of biblical learning there naturally came critical reviews and judgments. In answer to the critical storm deploring the tight use of language in the *New World Translation*, President Knorr explained:

> We do not discourage the use of any of these Bible versions, but we shall go on making suitable use of them. However, during all our years of using these versions we have found them defective. In one or another vital respect they are inconsistent or unsatisfactory, infected with religious traditions or worldly philosophy, and hence not in harmony with the sacred truths which Jehovah God has restored to his devoted people who call upon his name and seek to serve him with one accord.

Although most Witnesses have their own set of this translation of approved volumes for their own use in study, both privately and in the Kingdom Hall class sessions, they still use the King James Version in their house-to-house calling. There is no point, of course, in insisting on their own translation on their opening thrust. This can always be saved until the hearer and prospect is closer to the truth.

Among the many changes of direction, strategy, and program that President Knorr began was the use of music and singing. There had been some singing of old-time hymns during Pastor Russell's day. But Judge Rutherford had regarded singing as frivolous.

Their first book of "spiritual songs," as they prefer to call their hymns, did not appear until 1966. Prior to that time, whatever songs heard at Kingdom Hall meetings were the so-called Gospel songs, sung from collections printed by other Christian bodies. In fairness, one must bear in mind that the Jehovah's Witnesses do not regard themselves as a church. They are what their corporate title calls them—"The Watchtower Bible and Tract Society." Much of the negative criticism directed toward the Witnesses is directed at their failures and inconsistencies as a "church," the critic judging them according to conventional church patterns. The comparison does not work. The point of all this, in defense of the Witnesses' de-emphasis of music, is that they *are* primarily a Society, and not an ecclesiastical structure in the historic sense of the word. Even so, this small booklet of songs is presently quite adequate for their meeting needs. A liturgical order of worship makes little sense to them, anyway, and is not a necessity to their way of life.

Their new song book is entitled "Singing and Accompanying Yourselves with Music in Your Hearts." It is a collection of a hundred and eighteen songs. There are no credit lines for author or composer, although at least one song, number ten, was composed by a Brother King during his imprisonment in Africa in the late forties or early fifties. Brother King anonymously gives this song to the Witnesses and their Jehovah:

From house to house, from door to door, Jehovah's Word
    we spread,
From town to town, from farm to farm, Jehovah's "sheep"
    are fed.
This good news that God's kingdom rules, as Jesus Christ
    foretold,
Is being preached throughout the earth by Christians
    young and old.

. . . .

Of course, it's not at every door we find a hearing ear,
At times there is a scolding tongue and those who will not
    hear.
'Twas just the same in Jesus' day, not all would hear his
    word.

He said his "sheep" would hear his voice; hence we are not
    deterred.

Then let us go from door to door to spread the Kingdom
    news.

And whether they are "sheep" or "goats," we'll let the peo-
    ple choose.

At least we'll name Jehovah's name, his glorious truth
    declare,

And as we go from door to door, we'll find his "sheep" are
    there!

The omnipresent Twenty-third Psalm appears in the
Witness songbook, too. There are more versions and
paraphrases of this Psalm than all the others put together.
In this critic's opinion, the Witness version holds up much
better than the one used for years by the Plymouth
Brethren in colonial days. In their day they were con-
sidered masters of the paraphrase of Psalmody. Here is
Psalm Twenty-three from the Witness Songbook:

Jehovah God is my shepherd; so why should I fear or fret?

For he who cares for his sheep so much, will none of his own
    forget.

By quiet waters he leads me; my soul does restore and
    bless.

He guides my steps for his own name's sake in pathways of
    righteousness.

Tho' in the vale of deep shadow I walk, I need fear no harm,

For my Great Shepherd is always near; his staff keeps me
    from alarm.

My head with oil he refreshes; my cup he has filled up well.

His loving kindness will follow me, and e'er in his house I'll
    dwell.

They also have their "battle songs," the following being
representative:

True servants of Jehovah God, there is much work to do.
A prophecy must be fulfilled that now applies to you.
You must pour out its seven plagues on Babylon the Great
And all the rest of Satan's crowd, warn them of their sure
    fate.

The first plague pour upon the "earth," where ulcers will
    appear
On men who bow before the "beast" and who its "image"
    fear.
The second plague pour on the "sea"; the radicals expose
The third on many waters shows how blood-guilt brings on
    woes.

The fourth plague pour upon the "sun," which scorches
    men with fire.
The fifth pour on the "wild beast's throne"; from pain let
    men perspire.
The sixth must fall upon the "stream," the "River
    Euphrates."
Its waters shall be all dried up, "Kings of the East" to
    please.

The seventh plague pour on the "air," the spirit of this
    world,
Which drives men to oppose God till hard truths like hail
    are hurled.
The privilege to pour these plagues will never come again;
So let us join to pour them out and save repentant men.

It isn't all blood-and-thunder with the Jehovah's
Witnesses:

> Once with confusion our sad hearts were filled,
> Drinking the cup false religion distilled.
> But with what happiness our hearts were thrilled,
> When of God's kingdom we heard!

Take sides with Jehovah; make him your delight,
He'll never forsake you, walk e'er in his light.
Tell the glad tidings of freedom and peace,
His rule by Christ Jesus will ever increase!

There have been many changes in the ways of the
Witnesses under Nathan Knorr's leadership. The hostility
toward church has diminished during his almost
anonymous reign. The anti-clericalism is gone. There is no
more picketing of churches on Sunday mornings. There are
no more cartoons and caricatures of clergy in the issues of
The Watchtower and *Awake!*

But in case anyone nurtures the idea that Knorr has
backed away from the original cause and purpose of the
Jehovah's Witnesses, this emphatically is not the case. A
true and faithful steward, he has used his gifts and insights
for the furtherance of the aims and purposes of Jehovah's
Witnesses. He has continued the policy of encouraging the
Witnesses to defend and protect their civil rights. He has
only reduced the noise level of the Witnesses' causes. He
was the first Witness leader to grasp the public relations
value of having the huge assembly, now exceeding a
quarter of a million people at a time. This is all the more
remarkable in this day when big-time sports spectaculars
claim attendance figures considerably under 100,000. One
of the lasting effects of the meeting of the Witnesses in
Yankee Stadium more than fifteen years ago was the
astonishing spectacle of finding the stadium seats and
grounds completely clear of litter on the following morning.
The Witnesses had organized and swept out the place after
more than 250,000 of the faithful had departed! Management shook its corporate head in disbelief. That is one-
upmanship in its finest hour!

In spite of his seeming anonymity, President Knorr holds
his time free for a few minutes after every meal when he is

in the refectory to listen to problems and to listen to suggestions. He declines interviews for the media, preferring to go his quiet but extremely effective and efficient way with the Society before him. He holds absolute power. Not even the various corporation directors or board members serve as either checks or balances. No matter, now. He has given a good account of his stewardship. Confidently he expects Armageddon to begin by the time he is ready to step down as the last in the line.

6

Paradise Lost and Armageddon Delayed— the Jehovah's Witness Cosmogony and Theology

According to Jehovah's Witness doctrine, this is how and where it all began:

Now it came to be the day when the sons of the true God entered to take their station before Jehovah, and even Satan proceeded to enter right among them. Then Jehovah said to Satan: "Where do you come from?" At that Satan answered Jehovah and said: "From roving about in the earth and from walking about in it." And Jehovah went on to say to Satan: "Have you set your heart upon my servant Job, that there is no one like him in the earth, a man blameless and upright, fearing God and turning aside from bad?" At that Satan answered Jehovah and said: "Is it for nothing that Job has feared God? Have not you yourself put up a hedge about him and about his house and about everything that he has

75

all around? The work of his hands you have blessed, and his livestock itself has spread abroad in the earth. But, for a change, thrust out your hand, please, and touch everything he has and see whether he will not curse you to your very face." Accordingly Jehovah said to Satan: "Look! Everything that he has is in your hand. Only against him himself do not thrust out your hand!" So Satan went out away from the person of Jehovah.

—Job 1:6-12, NWT

From information gleaned from isolated texts spread here and there throughout Scripture, Charles Taze Russell concluded that Jehovah also gave Satan six thousand years to seduce and destroy not only Job, who was number one, but *all* the succeeding generations of men. If he (Satan) does not get the job done in that allotted time, then Jehovah will step in, through his son Jesus (who was the archangel Michael prior to coming to earth), and chain Satan for the thousand years of peace. After this time he will be loosed for a short time and then destroyed, and all his evil works with him. The destruction includes all those beings both in spirit and human who have been unrepentantly seduced by the Evil One.

From this excerpt from the Book of Job (plus texts chosen here and there in Scripture) Russell and his immediate successor, Judge Rutherford, developed the doctrines that characterize this extraordinary chapter in the history of religious bodies.

In the Jehovah's Witness teaching about creation, the heavens are regarded as having existed long before earth and the stars and the other planets. Heaven is where the angels live. They are known as "spirit-creatures." They were first created by Jehovah and then appointed to various assignments to look after the various and myriad forms of life. Each form of life "has a spirit in it."

Explained in a modern and popular comparative, Jehovah is the Chairman of the Board. Jesus is the Executive President, followed by the hosts of angels, or "home office staff." Man, being lower than the angels, is next in the hierarchy but considerably farther down in the scale and more distant from the angelic hosts than the hosts are from Jesus or Jehovah. Man is the head of woman, who is a step still farther away from Jehovah, who is the center of life. Animal life runs in fifth place on the racetrack of creation. Vegetation is several paces behind the preceding order. In all this structure, heaven is the seat of cosmic government and the capital of creation.

When Jehovah created the earth and placed life upon it, he put one of his super-angels, or archangels, in charge. It was his job to see to it that everything lived in harmony and cadence with each other, and therefore in tune with Jehovah's purpose in the first place. This angel, Lucifer—whose name was changed to Satan after his fall from grace—had a large company of lesser angels to assist him in carrying out the desires and plans of Jehovah. When this arrangement began, the earth consisted solely of the Garden of Eden and had as its sole human occupants no others than Adam and Eve.

The guardian, or super-angel, soon found that his appointment as overseer was heady stuff, indeed. Power begins to corrupt him. He starts having ideas on how he can rearrange and improve things to his own benefit, or so goes his thinking and fantasizing. In the disguise of a serpent, he manages to sweet-talk Adam and Eve into worshipping him instead of Jehovah God. This was easily accomplished through the woman. Next he turns his sweet reasonableness and charm upon his colleagues, the next lower rank of angels that had been appointed as his assistants. They were also seduced. Now known as Satan the "Opposer," Lucifer took over control of both heaven and earth, the two together being the oldest and original perfect creation.

Paradise was lost. The fallen angels were now damned. That is, they became demons. Adam and Eve were exiled. This latter action was carried out by cherub angels, under the command of Jehovah, who had remained loyal to him. This is the story of how evil came to be and what happened to the human race that has made man so wicked and dangerous. Satan and his demonic forces are still in charge of the earth, although they were driven out of heaven in 1914, the year the reign of King Jesus began there. The news of this announced restoration and the beginning of the thousand year reign of peace was given to mankind through Pastor Russell and his successors.

Jehovah is now making final preparations to regain his lost world, the earth. How this will be done, and what effects it will have, are described by certain scriptural passages in Isaiah, Daniel, and Revelation, as well as the "Little Apocalypse" of the synoptic Gospels. There must also be included that dramatic passage from Zechariah 14 and its vivid description of men rotting on their feet as their eyeballs fall out on the pavement. There are also certain descriptive passages of the end that are recorded in Ezekiel, which the Witnesses present as isolated evidence of what the end of Jehovah's anger will shortly produce.

The question frequently comes up, why didn't Jehovah nip this rebellion in the bud at its very beginning? Why didn't he cut the infection out while it was still localized and before its cancerous growth had produced so much suffering and death? The Witnesses admit that Jehovah *could* have done this. However, Jehovah's delay is explained.

For a moment, pretend that you are Jehovah. You are

faced with this particular problem of disloyalty and down-right treason and the betrayal of a trust on the part of one of your highest assistants. You can, of course, give the order for his capture and execution. But what would the angelic hosts think? Would they think that you acted quickly so as to prevent a confrontation in which you might possibly get the worst of it? "Look in the Book of Job," the Witnesses tell us, "and read for yourself that Jehovah gave the devil his chance to steal Job from him."

To have Satan killed immediately, argue the Witnesses, would have been a sign of weakness, not of strength. When Satan flung down the gauntlet, Jehovah had no choice but to accept the defiant challenge. However, Jehovah did set a time limit on how long he would put up with Satan's attempt to prove that he was stronger than Jehovah God. Jehovah's reasoning was that a contest was brought by the claims of Satan as to who was supreme. You, still trying to react as Jehovah would, decide to give him 6,000 years to gain the victory. This victory is defined with the un-derstanding that Satan must have *all* the people worship him in that space of time. There are to be no exceptions. The 6,000 years are now up. Even after all these years of Satan trying to prove his point, he has not succeeded. The issue of world domination is now nearly settled. Satan and his forces have been expelled from heaven by Jesus and the good angels. The earth is next.

In spite of all the efforts of Satan and his evil hosts of demons, together they were never able to make all men submit. For instance, Abel never submitted. He was thereby the first Witness of Jehovah. Since his day, there have always been Jehovah's Witnesses. This list of worthies includes all the prophets of old and the great spiritual leaders of Israel. We are referred to Scripture:

So, then, because we have so great a cloud of

> witnesses surrounding us, let us also put off every
> weight and the sin that easily entangles us, and
> let us run with endurance the race that is set
> before us, as we look intently at the Chief Agent
> and Perfecter of our faith, Jesus.
> —Hebrews 12:1-2, NWT

Christians are being watched by that cloud of witnesses
from ages past. This encourages us to perform acts of faith.

The Jehovah's Witnesses consider themselves part of an
unbroken line of faithful men and women that reaches
back in history to the time of Abel, the first Witness. It is
their version of an "apostolic succession," in a certain
sense. And even as the historic churches, such as the
Orthodox churches of the east, the Roman Catholic and
the Anglican churches in the west, claim an unbroken line
back to Jesus himself, and through Him back to Aaron and
Moses, so too do the Witnesses regard their spiritual
ancestry. Like the others, they also admit that the line
became rather shaky and almost indeterminate from time
to time in days of crisis, but that it survived intact. For instance, that period between the writing of the Old and the
New Testaments was about four hundred years long. There
is no information on who the Witnesses were during those
troubled times.

> Though weakly at times, the gospel torch con-
> tinued to burn throughout the centuries un-
> quenched by religion's flood of opposition.
> Faithful Witnesses of Jehovah continued to
> triumph over religion, by God's grace.
> —*Theocratic Aid to Kingdom Publishers* (1945)

During that seemingly interminable six thousand years
of Satan's futile attempts to get all of humanity to worship

him, Jehovah was not idle nor off somewhere else involved in more interesting pursuits and pastimes. He was making plans for what he would do when Satan had exhausted his desire and attempts to be independent of and superior to the godhead. Jehovah considered that first of all he would need someone to replace Satan as guardian of the earth. He would need new helpers to replace the demons, the fallen angels.

Jehovah decided to replace Satan with his own son, Jesus, who had so admirably and completely proved himself by His perfect life and death. Knowing our problems through his own earthly life, he would prove to be the answer to all the problems of both man *and* Jehovah. God decided to use men as a replacement for the fallen angels, one hundred and forty-four thousand of them. They were to be redeemed and sent on to heaven to replace the banished demons. The new earth would be made up of all the rest of mankind.

It is generally understood in the Witness scheme of things that the Old Testament prophets, patriarchs, and other worthies are not numbered among the 144,000 simply because chronologically they were born too soon.

Only those who have lived since Christ are eligible to become members of the remnant that are destined and decreed by Jehovah to assist Jesus in ruling the heavens. Old Testament martyrs will be resurrected to life on earth. This is not their fault. The time problem simply prevents them from being candidates for the heavenly elite. From this belief apparently sprung the belief that prompted Judge Rutherford to buy that large house in San Diego for the patriarchs to live in when they returned to earth to supervise the post-Armageddon clean-up. This is expected to take seven months of plain hard work for the surviving Jehovah's Witnesses. When that disagreeable but triumphant task has been completed, then Eden will have been restored and the thousand year reign of peace will have begun, free from suffering, death, and the plague of Satan and his demonic hosts.

So we come to understand that the Jehovah's Witnesses, by themselves, have kept the light shining in the darkness down through the corridor of the years and through the halls of time. If they had not remained loyal and steadfast to Jehovah God, his cause would have been lost. Satan would have seduced everybody and thus would have won his wager with the Lord made back in Job's day. Except for the Witnesses, evil would have triumphed in that classic battle between Satan and Jehovah, and God would be no more.

This view of history as a contest between Jehovah and Satan—actually an extension of the role of Lucifer in the Book of Job—has some inevitable conclusions in thought. Jehovah is not responsible for the world's misery. Satan is at the bottom of it. The Witnesses insist that Jehovah is all-powerful and loving. Yet at the same time, Jehovah God has been watching this terrible spectacle of misery, suffering, and death for *six thousand years* without lifting a hand to help his children—toward whom he is supposed to be just, loving, and merciful. It is not regarded as reprehensible that Jehovah had his angelic hosts available to stop the carnage at his command. The Witness sees it as natural and fair for Jehovah not to interfere in the personal struggle between Himself and one of His great but lesser creations, an archangel. When the question is raised as to why the Witness believes that Jehovah has delayed Armageddon for 6,000 years the answer is that Jehovah decided to stay by the time schedule that Scripture reveals to all who will seek it. Behind this there is, of course, the argument that Jehovah was absolutely determined to vindicate Himself, and this was a first consideration. The desire that

Jehovah has to bring salvation to man obviously comes in second.

Jehovah, through His actions, can now proclaim throughout the whole cosmos that He is supreme and that He alone stands in control over all. His name has been cleared. Now it is time for Job and his race of human beings to have their sufferings removed—sufferings caused by the now-vanquished evil one. And how does he set about relieving the suffering of humanity? He sets up the battle of Armageddon in order to destroy ninety-nine percent of those who were victimized by Satan and who have not returned to the true worship of Jehovah God.

The Witness view of the history of religion (especially Christianity) since the time of Jesus is a seemingly senseless and endless tale of suffering and woe. There has been naught but the continuous falling away from the truth and corruption of Jehovah's commands and wishes. This slide downhill was arrested in 1872 by the appearance of Charles Taze Russell. Through him and by him and his tiny band of followers, the false garments of religion were stripped off and the original faith once more became visible in the teachings of the Jehovah's Witnesses.

The doctrine of God, according to the Witnesses, begins with a clarification of his names. He is known especially, and preferably, as "Jehovah," which means "the Self-existing One." He is also known as Elohim, a Hebrew plural word for God. These two names of God are meant to refer to God in two ways, one as creator and one as redeemer.

Jehovah is a spirit-being. He is *not* a spirit-creature. That is, he has always existed uncreated. However, there was a time before creation when He was all alone in space, but He wasn't really lonesome because He is self-contained and doesn't lack anything. Finally, He began to create. He began stirring. His Spirit "moved" Him. Since then His effects have been felt, and His power, but being a Spirit, He will always be invisible to man—which is just as well, because man could not stand up to His Blazing Presence if He showed Himself in His fullness to man.

The word "Spirit," translated from the Hebrew root, comes out "wind." From here it is explained that wind is invisible to man, *and* it has power. A more accurate definition of the word than "wind" is "breath." But this word is imprecise to the Witness. The word "breath" is too gentle. To them it takes away the sense of mighty power and force.

Although the main attributes of God are love, wisdom, justice, and power, and the Witness teachings insist that the most important of these attributes is love, yet, when one studies Witness doctrine as a whole, one sees much more evidence of His power and justice than one does of wisdom and love, certainly by New Testament standards.

Judge Rutherford explained in *The Harp of God* that God's justice showed itself by inflicting punishment on violators of His laws. He makes clear that this has shown itself time and again throughout history in such cataclysmic events as the Flood, the destruction of Sodom and Gomorrah, the Exodus, and the destructions of Jerusalem, not only during the reign of Hezekiah, but during other times too. The Judge, in *The Harp of God,* also noted many other events that he had culled from the Old Testament—the "Hebrew Scriptures," as he and subsequent Witnesses preferred to call the Old Testament.

Justice was thus meted out through His power. His love appears in the sacrifice of "the dearest treasure of His heart," His beloved Son, that mankind may have a chance for eternal life. His wisdom reveals itself chiefly in His Great Plan, in which He gradually permits man to see more and more clearly as Armageddon draws near. He is so wise that from the very beginning He knew how it would all turn out. And now, in our day, we are blessed with the fullness of revelation to man of His total plan which has been made plain through His Witnesses. Through them humanity learns of Jehovah's judgment and wrath, mainly, and not so much about wisdom and love.

Jehovah is free to spare the sinner *only* in harmony with the Divine Plan. There is an immeasurable and uncrossable gulf between Jehovah and mankind. God alone is immortal. Death is impossible for Him. No other creature is endowed with immortality. Jehovah is going to change this condition upon the restoration of Eden. He has already given men hope for the endless life in the new heavens which He is about to create.

All creation naturally revolves around Him as its life source and creative center. Everything is inseparably tied to Him. Because of this He is deeply involved in the tragic human situation of struggling against sin and evil. The Witnesses perceive that the beginning of God's plan was to place all creatures, both in heaven and on earth, into a harmonious structure of peace and order so that it may fulfill His will.

Jehovah is about to regain His plundered planet and wrench it free from Satan's grasp. He will accomplish this by destroying all his enemies in both heaven and earth. His emerging theocratic government, of which the Jehovah's Witness structure and polity is the forerunner, will govern all creation. His justice will prevail. It will be carried out in divine wrath to a total degree that will make any further rebellions impossible to achieve. All souls who expect to live eternally must submit to His heavenly Son, who will be made the theocratic king in that great day, having a theocratic government to implement it. If and when a person can accept this idea, then his eternal life and happiness are almost assured.

From this point in belief, one can easily conclude that all governments, all human doings and commerce, are doomed to destruction. This includes all churches and all religions. They will simply disintegrate before the onslaught of the legions of a wrathful Jehovah God. The final triumph over Satan is certain and imminent. All his works are coming to nothing in this day. Satan himself has gone as far as he can go. His destruction is upon him. His evil shall soon disappear from the face of the earth forever! The post-Armageddon world will be one in which evil cannot possibly intrude its presence, for it shall have been finally destroyed by the power of Jehovah God.

Like most millennial-minded groups, the Witnesses look upon history as a long series of horizontal or lateral events that have been foreordained by God to happen in the order that they have happened. History seems to be looked upon as a "clothesline" version of chronology. Events from creation on are strung out like washing on a line. In our day Jehovah has come to the end of the clothesline of foreordained history. He knew all the time how large the wash was and how long the clothesline had to be in order to get the job done. He will now take down the washing, including the clothesline and the poles. Never again will there ever be even a rag of man's sin and rebellion to be laundered. Satan will be the last one to be taken off the clothesline of history as we have known it, and that will be that.

With a little inquiry one can see that the Witness believes that whatever happens in history was appointed by Jehovah God to come about that way. Furthermore, any student of the Bible can come to some understanding of the ways of the Lord in history through this approach. But true knowledge and understanding of Jehovah's plan for creation can be understood and received only by a person who is free from prejudice, and who has become willing to adopt and utilize various scriptural helps as provided by *The Watchtower* and *Awake!*

There is no changing of Jehovah's mind or His plan. He has set the time and place for every one of His purposes to be worked out. When the time is ripe, He acts swiftly—no capricious or whimsical God here. When He does act, it is with immediate justice and with power—always power. Wisdom and love emerge and become dominant in times when the social and political stress of a nation is not acute. We can all remember as a child how we had to learn when to approach father for our own reasons. Timing was important. If one had been recently guilty of infraction of some family rule, and had been found out, then it was naturally better to wait a few days in order to give wisdom and love a good chance to replace wrath and justice. So it is with Jehovah. A gentle reminder is unearthed in the Book of Acts:

> He said to them: "It does not belong to you to get knowledge of the times or seasons which the Father has placed in his own jurisdiction; but you will receive power when the holy spirit arrives upon you, and you will be witnesses of me both in Jerusalem, and in all Judea and Samaria and to the most distant part of the earth."
> —Acts 1:7-8, NWT

This verse also is interpreted to mean that the Witnesses possess the key for determining the calculations of Jehovah God, and that through them the timetable of the Lord may be discerned and made plain.

Following this line of thought, we begin by learning that in biblical and prophetic language, a day is not simply or necessarily twenty-four hours long. It is sometimes interpreted as a year. In figuring out dates, each "day" in Scripture is three hundred and sixty-five days long, at least as far as determining the big dates in history is concerned. This is supported by Ezekiel the prophet:

> A day for a year, a day for a year, is what I have given you . . .
>
> —Ezekiel 4:6 NWT

Shortly after the year 600 B.C.E., a great prophet appeared by the name of Daniel. This coincided with the time of Hebrew captivity in Babylon during the reign of Nebuchadnezzar. (He was the king of Babylon who probably, according to the text, lived for seven years as a vegetarian. This may have been for health reasons known best by the king and his physician, but it was regarded by the Hebrew slaves as a visitation of the divine judgment and wrath.)

Charles Taze Russell was utterly captivated by the Book of Daniel, using much of its content as a springboard into his total biblical explanations that followed through the years. Hence, in order to understand a little more clearly where Russell based his ideas, it is well to recount the story wherein Daniel saw a vision of Gentile rule as a great tree in the midst of the earth. All this is crucial to the eschatological structure of the Jehovah's Witnesses. Their view of the end of the world hangs much on this story:

> I, Nebuchadnezzar, happened to be at ease in my house and flourishing in my palace. There was a dream that I beheld, and it began to make me afraid. And there were mental images upon my bed and visions of my head that began to frighten me. And from me an order was being put through to bring in before me all the wise men of Babylon, that they might make known to me the very interpretation of the dream.
>
> At that time the magic-practicing priests, the

conjurers, the Chaldeans and the astrologers were entering; and I was saying before them what the dream was, but its interpretation they were not making known to me. And at last there came in before me Daniel, whose name is Belteshazzar according to the name of my god and in whom there is the spirit of the holy gods; and before him I said what the dream was:

"O Belteshazzar the chief of the magic-practicing priests, because I myself well know that the spirit of the holy gods is in you and that there is no secret at all that is troubling you, tell me the visions of my dream that I have beheld and its interpretation.

"Now the visions of my head upon my bed I happened to be beholding, and, look! a tree in the midst of the earth, the height of which was immense. The tree grew up and became strong, and its very height finally reached the heavens, and it was visible to the extremity of the whole earth. Its foliage was fair, and its fruit was abundant, and there was food for all on it. Under it the beast of the field would seek shade, and on its boughs the birds of the heavens would dwell, and from it all flesh would feed itself.

"I continued beholding in the visions of my head upon my bed, and, look! a watcher, even a holy one, coming down from the heavens themselves. He was calling out loudly, and this is what he was saying: 'Chop the tree down, and cut off its boughs. Shake off its foliage, and scatter its fruitage. Let the beast flee from under it, and the birds from its boughs. However, leave its rootstock itself in the earth, even with a banding of iron and of copper, among the grass of the field; and with the dew of the heavens let it be wet, and with the beast let its portion be among the vegetation of the earth. Let its heart be changed from that of mankind, and let the heart of a beast be given to it, and let seven times pass over it. By the decree of watchers the thing is, and by the saying of holy ones the request is, to the intent that people living may know that the Most High is Ruler in the kingdom of mankind and that to the one whom he wants to, he gives it and he sets up over it even the lowliest one of mankind.'

"This was the dream that I myself, King Nebuchadnezzar, beheld; and you yourself, O Belteshazzar, say what the interpretation is, forasmuch as all the other wise men of my kingdom are unable to make known to me the interpretation itself. But you are competent, because the spirit of the holy god is in you."

At that time Daniel himself, whose name is Belteshazzar, was astonished for a moment, and his very thoughts began to frighten him.

The king was answering and saying, "O Belteshazzar, do not let the dream and the interpretation themselves frighten you."

Belteshazzar was answering and saying, "O my lord, may the dream apply to those hating you, and its interpretation to your adversaries.

"The tree that you beheld, that grew great and became strong and the height of which finally reached the heavens and which was visible to all the earth, and the foliage of which was fair, and the fruit of which was abundant, and on which there was food for all; under which the beasts of the field would dwell, and on the boughs of which the birds of the heavens would reside, it is you, O king, because you have grown great and become strong, and your grandeur has grown great and reached the heavens, and your rulership to the extremity of the earth.

"And because the king beheld a watcher, even a holy one, coming down from the heavens, who was also saying: 'Chop the tree down, and ruin it. However, leave its rootstock itself in the earth, but with a banding of iron and of copper, among the grass of the field,

"And because the king beheld a watcher, even a holy one, coming down from the heavens, who was also saying: 'Chop the tree down, and ruin it. However, leave its rootstock itself in the earth, but with a banding of iron and of copper, among the grass of the field, and with the dew of the heavens let it become wet, and with the beasts of the field let its portion be until seven times themselves pass over it,' this is the interpretation, O king, and the decree of the Most High is that which must befall my lord the king. And you they will be driving away from men, and with the beasts of the field your dwelling will come to be, and the vegetation is what they will give even to you to eat just like bulls; and with the dew of the heavens you yourself will be getting wet, and seven times themselves will pass over you, until you know that the Most High is Ruler in the kingdom of mankind, and that to the one whom he wants to he gives it.

"And because they said to leave the rootstock of the tree, your kingdom will be sure to you after you know that the heavens are ruling. Therefore, O king, may my counsel seem good to you, and remove your own sins by righteousness, and your iniquity by showing mercy to the poor ones. Maybe there will occur a lengthening of your prosperity."

All this befell Nebuchadnezzar the king.

—Daniel 4:4-28, NWT

Here follows the interpretation that Charles Taze Russell made of this passage, of which he was so deeply enamored and influenced:

Daniel, chapter four, showed that God's kingdom would not be set up until the end of the seven times of the Gentile nations under their invisible overlord, Satan. Because of the controversy over Jehovah's supremacy and universal domination, God delegated to Satan, the devil, a limited period of time. In that period God's adversary would have uninterrupted rule over the world. Such a period without interruption would terminate the "seven times" of the Gentile powers. Those "seven times" ended in October 1914 C.E.

To summarize: Charles Taze Russell, in his search for the key to the Scriptures—especially any parts that would shed light on the end of the Gentile times—came up with this much:

A day equals one year. A "time" means a year of 360 days. Now seven "times" would be $7 \times 360 = 2520$. Therefore, Gentile supremacy and Jewish slavery ended 2,520 years after 606 B.C.E., the date of Nebuchadnezzar's dream and Daniel's prophetic explanation. This brings us up to 1914 C.E.

This is the year that Satan and his angels were cut down from heaven, and Christ enthroned, paradise regained.

This date marks the beginning of the Second Coming. This date sets the stage for Armageddon. Consequently, this date marks the end of the present world system and the beginning of the end of time itself.

Moreover, the Witnesses estimate that it is about 5,939 years since the creation of Adam. They estimate that according to Genesis 5, the span between Adam and the date of Noah's flood was 1,656 years. This figure is determined by counting the years from Adam's creation to the birth of Seth, then grandson Enos down to the birth of Noah, plus the years that Noah lived *up to* the flood. They further declare that the time between the Flood and the time of God's promise to Abraham was 427 years, if one figures from Genesis 11 and 12. From this time until the crossing of the Red Sea was an additional 430 years. Through listed chronology and time elapse, by biblical counting, it is determined that 1,945 years pass between Abraham and the year 1 B.C.E. So now, finally, if the figures are correctly added up, one comes out with a figure of 5,939 years from the creation of Adam until 1914.

This chronology was prepared by Charles Taze Russell in the nineteenth century and published in his book, *The New Heavens and the New Earth.*

The Witnesses, as we have seen, do not accept the idea of the Trinity. With a slight gleam of triumphant one-upmanship in their eyes, they point out that the word "Trinity" does not occur in Scripture. Russell was right on that score. The use of the word "Trinity" has been traced back no further than the second century, when the word appeared in a polemic address given by the Bishop of Antioch in Syria when he was writing and preaching in defense of the Faith. This precedent was followed so frequently that it became an issue at the Council of Nicaea in 325 C.E.

What the King James Version has in 1 John 5:7 is:

> For there are three that bear record in heaven,
> the Father, the Word, and the Holy Ghost: and
> these three are one.

The Revised Standard Version reads:

> There are three witnesses, the Spirit, the water,
> and the blood.

The *New World Translation* of the Jehovah's Witnesses
reads:

> For there are three witness bearers, the spirit and
> the water and the blood, and the three are in
> agreement.

The Witnesses insist that the verse in the King James Version is spurious, and certain biblical scholars have traced this passage to a point no earlier than the sixth century C.E. This particular passage did not find its way into a Greek manuscript of this epistle until the middle of the 1400s. Hence, the Jehovah Witness denial of the validity of the doctrine of the Trinity on scriptural grounds is accurate. In any case, they insist that the doctrine is altogether foreign to true Christianity.

The idea of a god in three persons is too much for the Witnesses. They consider the whole idea repugnant. As Pastor Russell declared in *Let God Be True*:

> God-fearing persons who want to know Jehovah
> and serve Him find it a bit difficult to love and
> worship a complicated, freakish looking, three-
> headed God. The clergy who inject such ideas
> will contradict themselves in their very next
> breath by stating that God created man in His

own image; and certainly no one has *seen* a three-headed human creature.

The Witnesses also reject the idea of hell. In his time Judge Rutherford taught that the word "hell" is translated from the Hebrew word *Sheol*, which is the word used in the Hebrew Scriptures (Old Testament). This word, he writes, is translated as "grave" on some occasions, and at other times, "pit." In the Christian Scriptures (New Testament), the same word, "hell," is a translation of the Greek word *hades*, the condition of death.

The Witnesses not only object to the pagan concept of hell as contained in Christian beliefs; they also give other reasons why a hell of torment is not included in Jehovah's scheme of things. It is not only unreasonable, they repeat, but it is contrary to justice, and it is incongruous with the attribute of love. Besides all that, it's unscriptural.

Putting the damper on any doctrine of eternal punishment, they proceed to an entirely different aspect, in which it is explained that Jesus Christ will preside over the judgment of Satan, his evil spirits, and the children of disobedience. The sentence, when it is finally pronounced, will be death from which there cannot be any resurrection, a clear case of conviction and sentencing before the trial. But they insist that there is so much evidence that further weighing of justice is unnecessary.

That part of humanity not among the disobedient children of God will survive the terrible cataclysm of Armageddon. Those faithful Witnesses who died prior to the Last Day will be resurrected to rejoin the faithful on earth in that paradise which will be plagued and cursed no longer with suffering, woes, sickness, and frustrations:

And he will wipe out every tear from their eyes, and death will be no more, neither will mourning

nor outcry nor pain be any more. The former
things have passed away.
                          —Revelation 21:4, NWT

and

In his days the righteous one will sprout,
   And the abundance of peace until the moon is no more.
And he will have subjects from sea to sea
   And from the River to the ends of the earth.
Before him the inhabitants of waterless regions will bow
      down.
   And his very enemies will lick the dust itself.
                          —Psalm 72:7-9, NWT

A secure, God-worshipping world it shall be, filled with
love and joy, not for a thousand years, nor a million or a
billion, but forever. So it is joyfully spread forth in *Let God
Be True.*

One of the chief difficulties that prospective converts
have with the Witness body of faith is accommodating
themselves to the teachings regarding the person of Jesus
Christ. While the Witnesses do indeed proclaim that
"Jesus is Lord," they do not mean by these words the same
thing that the various church affirmations of faith intend.
According to Witness literature, there was a time when
Jesus was not, a time when Jehovah was truly and absolutely alone; Jesus was the first creation of Jehovah.

Before Jesus' life on earth, He was a "spirit-creature"
called "Michael," the archangel:

And during that time Michael will stand up, the
great prince who is standing in behalf of the sons
of your people. And there will certainly occur a
time of distress such as has not been made to oc-

cur since there came to be a nation until that time. And during that time your people will escape, every one who is found written down in the book.

—Daniel 12:1, NWT

The name "Michael" means "who is like unto God." Therefore Jesus is a mighty one, and as such is properly called a "god," such as in the Gospel of John:

Do you say to me whom the Father sanctified and dispatched into the world, "You blaspheme," because I said, I am God's son?

—John 10:36, NWT

In essence, Jesus is regarded as the reincarnation of Michael the Archangel, and *is* Michael in human form.

The Witnesses also state that Jehovah alone had no beginning, and that therefore there was a time when Christ was not. He is the first creation of God, a short time before the creation of Adam. But inasmuch as there was a time when Christ was not, then He is not eternal. Through the Incarnation, the "spirit-creature" entered into humanity and became the perfect human being. He showed by His body and life what Adam was like before the Fall. Jesus was rewarded for His life of perfect obedience by being given a divine nature *afterwards.* Here is the scriptural support for the Witness teaching:

Keep this mental attitude in you that was also in Christ Jesus, who, although he was existing in God's form, gave no consideration to a seizure, namely, that he should be equal to God. No, but he emptied himself and took a slave's form and came to be in the likeness of men. More than that, when he found himself in fashion as a man,

he humbled himself and became obedient as far
as death, yes, death on a torture stake. For this
very reason also God exalted him to a superior
position and kindly gave him the name that is
above every other name, so that in the name of
Jesus every knee should bend of those in heaven
and those on earth and those under the ground,
and every tongue should openly acknowledge
that Jesus Christ is Lord to the glory of God the
Father.
—Philippians 2:5-11, NWT

So, Christ is the Logos or pre-existent Word. He is the
highest spirit-creature of Jehovah. In that sense Christ is *a*
"god." Christ is also *a* son of Jehovah and a brother of
Lucifer, the angel of light who fell from heaven and became
Satan, the prince of darkness. Jesus of Nazareth was
Christ divested of heavenly glory and rank, shed of what
divinity he may have had as a "spirit-creature," and was
nothing more or less than perfect man.

Jehovah God adopted Jesus Christ when He was baptized by John. His resurrection is the bestowal of immortality and divinity given to Him as a reward for His
faithfulness. Also after the resurrection, He became a high
priest "after the order of Melchisedec," and an angel of the
New Covenant that replaced the promise that Jehovah had
given to Abraham. After Armageddon, Jesus and the
Church—which consists of 144,000—will rule the heavens.
As we have seen, all other Jehovah's Witnesses who cannot
possibly be numbered among that 144,000 will nevertheless
receive immortality and everlasting life, being resurrected
to life on earth, which will be made into a restored Garden
of Eden. So, one need not worry because he was born too
late to be chosen as one of the elect, for he too shall have
his reward, even though he will not be privileged to reign in

heaven with Jesus during the millennial age which is imminently upon us.

Jesus Christ, being a "spirit-creature," and hence made in the image of God before any other creatures were made, had at least the distinction of being created first, apparently as an archangel. He was made supervisor and director for all His father's work in the fashioning of a new earth. He was always faithful and true, hence His reward of superimposed divinity *after* the resurrection. Jesus was the instrument used whereby other spirit-beings came into existence. When Jehovah said, "let us make man in our image," He was talking to His Son who was on hand to cooperate in the completing of creation. This very neatly solves the problem of the use of the plural ending in the noun, *Elohim*, meaning "gods," in Genesis.

The Witnesses have no problem accepting the idea of the Virgin Birth, inasmuch as it is apparently true, according to Scripture and is consistent with the way that they read it. Mary is regarded as being "highly favored" and blessed among women:

> Good day, highly favored one, Jehovah is with you.
>
> —Luke 1:28, NWT

The Witnesses insist, of course, that she could not possibly be the mother of God, as is implied in certain Greek texts using the word *theotokos* (god-bearer). It is explained that the Logos, Jesus' life-force, was put into the ovum in the womb of the unmarried Mary so that she (with her free consent preceding the act) could thereby provide for the human body of Jesus. The body of Jesus is regarded as physically perfect because Adam was not the ancestral father, but the Logos or Word was, the life-giver, Jehovah. This force from God is called the "Holy Spirit." It (not

"He") kept Jesus' body free from sin even though it was developed in the body of a woman who was a descendant from Adam and Eve.

Jesus' main purpose in coming to earth in the form of a man was to challenge and defeat Satan, who claimed (Job 1:8-12) that not even Jehovah God can put a creature on earth who will follow His laws faithfully—if Satan and his demons get a chance to work him over. Jesus kept His integrity and defeated Satan, not only as recorded in the story of the struggle on the Mount of Temptation (Luke 4:1-14), but through His entire life of obedience to Jehovah, even in death. Jesus, by His perfect life and death, *earned* His place as King of Zion.

Through the life and death of Jesus Christ, Jehovah was now able to provide a King upon whose shoulders the responsibility for the theocratic government-to-come shall fall. Through Jesus' life on earth He had proved and demonstrated that Satan was a fraud, a liar, a slanderer, and a false god. Jehovah was finally ready to establish a righteous government. The groundwork had been laid. The King had proved Himself equal to the appointment. Soon the New Rule would vindicate Jehovah's name before all the world.

There was a secondary purpose in Jehovah's plan that must not be confused with the primary one just stated. This second purpose was to ransom captive Israel and save mankind from death. Jesus did indeed come to earth to die in sacrifice to God His Father in order that death could be destroyed forever. Thus the elect and the righteous inherit eternal life in the world that Jehovah God has promised to create in His own good time—which is now at hand.

Through Jesus' resurrection, death was conquered in the sense that it no longer had a permanent hold upon its victims. Death was changed by Jesus to provide a suspension of existence, a period of deep unconsciousness and dreamless sleep—a cosmic sleep, if you will—exclusively for those who have been elected to have their consciousness restored to them for life unending, right here on earth, the restored Eden.

The baptism of Jesus is regarded by the Witnesses as the act of consecration of Himself to the work which Jehovah God set before Him to accomplish. Immediately after the baptism (according to Matthew 3:13-17), Jesus was anointed by the Holy Spirit as He came up out of the Jordan River.

Jesus was led by the Spirit into the wilderness to be tempted by Satan. They regard the temptations exactly and completely as Scripture relates them. They were looked upon as a test of His devotion to Jehovah and the divine purpose. Thus He proved Himself to be Jehovah's *chief* Witness.

In Christian history there have been many theories of a doctrine of the Atonement. One can pick and choose from among several flavors. The Witnesses hold to a version of the atonement that is very much like the substitution theory. This one means that through Adam's fall, man is helpless against the powers of darkness. He cannot, by his own efforts, set himself free from this blight. Because man has lost his human perfection and the sinless state, the divine wrath of Jehovah has been enkindled. God's justice demands and requires that sinners be punished. But man cannot atone enough for his sin by himself. He cannot raise the full ransom price, for this is the same as that which was lost in Adam's fall, and one man cannot possibly do all that for *all* men.

The Witnesses say that the ransom was owed to Jehovah and that it was paid in full by the perfect life and death of Jesus. Thereby the equivalent to that which was lost by Adam in the Fall has been returned. Redemption is now available to all those who will avail themselves of it. All that is required is obedience to the requirements of Jesus, and faith in Him. The reward is the restoration and gift of a perfect human nature *and* the ability to survive Armageddon. These persons are known as "Jonadabs," and have been since Rutherford's day. They are the non-elect believers, that is, not eligible for the elite of 144,000. Tangibly, this means that if you have departed this life before Armageddon, your consciousness will be restored to you on that great day and you will live forever on this very same earth, which will have been remade into a planet that is finally free from disease, sickness, decay, and death in *all* forms of life.

Witness literature explains that Jesus began making the ransom payments at His baptism and that He continued to make regular installments throughout His whole ministry. Like so many modern-day mortgages, there was a balloon note at the end that could either be paid off at once, or by negotiating for a new mortgage for the balance. By the giving of His life, the last of the debt of mankind was paid by Him. Jesus could not make use of the ransom price Himself, but Jehovah did give Him His life back as a reward for faithfulness in fulfilling the Law and satisfying divine justice. It should be made clear that although humanity was liberated, this act did not include Adam himself. He died and stayed dead because Jehovah could not reverse His judgment like a human judge does, sometimes.

After Jesus' death, He spent the Sabbath resting in hell—the "grave." The Spirit of Jehovah materialized Him in a body that looked like an earthly body even though it was a spiritual body. Jehovah allowed this so that He could prove to the disciples, and for Scripture, that He had indeed returned life to Jesus as a reward for His loyalty. Now Jesus is both Lord and Christ, which He was not prior to the resurrection. Now He is the owner of everything and has the power and authority to carry out Jehovah's plan for Him.

He remained on earth for the next forty days after the resurrection, at which time He presented the full ransom price to Jehovah. The Witnesses make it clear that the kingdom was not yet set up or even organized. Jesus and the faithful were going to have to wait for 1,900 years, until the end of the times of the Gentiles, which as Pastor Russell figured, came about in October of 1914. Jesus waited patiently all that time for His enthronement. Although it happened without any excitement on earth over it, yet it *did* occur in heaven. Matters have been put to right there, at last. Now we watch the closing down of history as Armageddon moves closer and closer to the present hour and the lights of civilization go out one by one.

All of this is to be followed by the thousand-year reign on a renewed earth. Then Jehovah will once again turn Satan loose to test the faithful. Some (nobody knows how many) will be seduced by Satan and then he will be finally annihilated. The remaining steadfast ones will go on living on the earth forever, although there will not be any more children, because the earth would become overcrowded. One cannot help but suspect that Satan could turn out to be a great population regulator by leading people on to their destruction. When he is finally out of power, infertility may well be the only way to balance the population. It also raises an interesting and unanswered question: at what age does one stop aging in eternity? Do babies stay babies? Does an old man stay at, say, 85 years of age forever while others are "frozen" in adolescence for eternity? We trust that Jehovah, in His wisdom, has worked out this problem.

The process whereby the members of the new Church for heaven were selected began at Pentecost, the day the Holy Spirit lit upon the apostles ten days after Jesus had left their midst on Ascension Day. This process has continued slowly ever since that day. The total final number of church members has been fixed in the Book of Revelation at 144,000:

> And I heard the number of those who were sealed, a hundred and forty-four thousand, sealed out of every tribe of the sons of Israel.
> —Revelation 7:4, NWT

To this is added:

> And you made them to be a kingdom and priests to our God, and they will rule as kings over the earth.
> —Revelation 5:10, NWT

However, there are also other classes of believers. While not of the original elect of 144,000, yet they will be resurrected to an endless life on earth without pain or suffering. These are the Jonadabs, of previous reference. They are named after the Old Testament character who renounced Baal. They are regarded as "saved," but they do not have any rank. Then too, there are those referred to as "the other sheep." These have acknowledged Jesus as the Good Shepherd, as recorded in the Gospel of John 10:16. Both of these classes inherit eternal life on earth.

The Jehovah's Witnesses do not believe that Jehovah either desires or expects them to convert the whole world. They believe that Jesus never did put salvation first during His ministry. He did not try desperately to save the world from deserved destruction. The purpose of the true church, from the Witness point of view, is to "preach the Triumphant Kingdom message throughout the world *as a witness to all nations.*" The purpose of this is to acquaint everybody with God's plan so that they will have no excuse when the calamity visits them. They can at least have the opportunity to be either a "Jonadab" or "one of the Little Flock of the Good Shepherd."

To this end the Witnesses teach and maintain two "rites" or "sacraments," called "ordinances": Baptism and the Lord's Supper.

While Baptism is not essential to salvation, nor is it a requirement that would necessarily qualify one for church membership, it does mark the individual as one who has thereby dedicated his life to the service of Jehovah and the acceptance of the obligations which this automatically imposes on the person. The act does not convey any mystical or spiritual powers or gifts, nor any special kind of grace.

The Baptism of the Spirit is quite another matter. This is reserved for those who are numbered among the final 144,000 who will reign together with King Jesus in heaven. This is called "spirit-baptism." Obviously not all Witnesses are eligible for this. The ranks of the heavenly administration are ostensibly closed, except for a very few yet to be added. The President of the Jehovah's Witnesses is naturally one who has a place reserved for him, and has in all likelihood received "spirit-baptism" although this cannot, of course, be verified by anybody.

In obedience to Jesus' command, the "Lord's memorial meal" is re-enacted on the anniversary of the fourteenth day of Nisan—the first Thursday after the first full moon of the spring equinox. This was the night of the original Lord's Supper in the upper room as recorded in all the Gospels. The officiant at this table may be any Witness. The "emblems" are unleavened bread and wine. This rite is not regarded as a sacrament, either. There is no theology of the nature of the eucharist. The Witnesses have no liturgy of any kind whatsoever. Although the table is open to all members of the Society, only a very small number ever make their communion. These are the ones who feel beyond any doubt that they are of the 144,000 elect. For Jonadabs or any of the "other sheep" to even presume to receive is unthinkable because they would be drinking judgment unto themselves. There are many congregations, who on this night of Nisan 14, meet together for the Memorial Meal who never have anyone who is presumptuous enough to include himself among the elite communicants of heaven.

In the body of belief of the Jehovah's Witnesses, there are principles or elements which certify to the truth of the teaching of the Society. Their first criterion is that every one of their beliefs must be supported and demonstrated by Scripture in terms of at least one proof-text. The second element that guides their doctrine is that their theology is completely based on the Bible, a variation on the theme that the Holy Scriptures are the finished work of God. He has spoken forever and with finality. Hence it contains all truths necessary. Further revelation is unnecessary. Jehovah has said it all. It contains all the answers that any objector could possibly raise. Their theology is also regarded as authoritative, and many would say that it is also authoritarian. That is, its source is beyond human invention. There are times when it is even beyond human understanding. But that's all right, explain the Witnesses, because Jehovah used men to write down for Him the facts that He believed it necessary to pass on to men, including all the wisdom that Jehovah chose to reveal. The Witnesses further insist that their body of belief is in complete harmony with Jehovah and what is known about Him through the Scriptures.

So, in spite of all the high-sounding phrases, the four criteria and so on, they all boil down to one principle, the infallibility of Scripture, and by implication, infallibility of Witness' doctrine.

Scripture is not used devotionally among the Witnesses

at Kingdom Hall meetings, except an occasional Psalm reading. It seems that unless a phrase or verse of Scripture has a prophecy, either apparent or hidden, then it has but little meaning to them and becomes nothing more than connective tissue between verses that can be called prophetic.

Systematic study of Scripture is not practiced, either. Selected spot passages and isolated texts grouped together are much preferred as a study. It is called Bible Study, and, in the narrow sense of the word, it is, although there are no extant texts that would help one to make a thorough verse-by-verse or chapter-by-chapter critical study of any book of the Bible. Those parts of Scripture that the Witnesses do know, they know exceedingly well. This gives them an advantage, because a member of a conventional Christian church generally doesn't know very much of the Bible, either Old or New Testament. A householder is at their mercy unless he is grounded in scriptural information. When they do come across an individual in their house-to-house work who shows that he is fairly knowledgeable on Bible matters, they evince a show of interest and curiosity, but it slows up their attack and strategy considerably.

Because of their emphasis on eschatology and the doctrines of the Four Last Things (Death, Judgment, Hell, and Heaven) there is no pastoral ministry exercised among them to amount to anything. Counsel or instruction on either spiritual or devotional matters is unobtainable except in the simplest attempts to feed occasional scriptural verses recalled at random to fit the situation. There can be no pastoral ministry in terms of a pastor-client relationship involving some difficult problem of a personal nature. The only help and therapy available, really, is to get busy in the Lord's work and everything will work itself out for the good of all. Many pressing matters in an individual's life are left up to God to solve.

It naturally follows that spiritual direction is not available. This is not often found in the mainline churches anymore either, although at least a search for a spiritual director will turn up someone who has the wisdom, love, and competency to assist a person in developing the life of the Spirit in the world of today. Among the Witnesses there is no mystical, ascetic, or devotional theology available.

The various ministries that are used in the lives of people, such as marrying and burying, are borrowed from outside sources. There is no healing ministry, no visitation of the sick, laying on of hands, or intercessory prayer. There is no sacrament of penance, ministry of reconciliation, or any way to receive forgiveness for sin.

To the outsider this must seem a rather grim business, a barren spiritual community. However, one must bear in mind that the Witnesses themselves do not regard themselves as a "church," but as a "Society." Even its corporate title, "The Watchtower Bible and Tract Society," defines its major work, that of spreading the information of the imminent end that he who will listen may adjust his life to fit the facts of reality as the Witness sees them. When one becomes all wrapped up and involved in the activism of this Society, all other things become faint and dim. Nothing else matters.

The Jehovah's Witness stands in strong relief against any and all religious groups that regard right belief as secondary to proper social action. He will have none of this. He is not about to take on the sufferings of others nor to ease their situations by social palliatives. Likewise, he stands out from any and all groups that maintain a ministry of the spirit and a sacramental life within a liturgical order of things. The Witness depends for his solace and security on his system of beliefs centering on prophecy and Armageddon. Belief is much more important that the improvement of either an individual's character or his life situation. Relationships with people out in the world where one makes a living are secondary. Salvation does not depend upon any particular kind of moral conduct, either before or after conversion. It depends simply upon the acceptance of the truth—as the Witness sees it.

The "truth" (i.e., Jehovah's Witness teachings) makes men free. It is the key that opens the door to all mystery and solves any and all problems. If a Witness becomes discouraged or falls ill, his malaise is not traced to the state of his *health* but to the state of his *belief*. The possibility of a gland dysfunction, a wrong diet, a stressful job situation, or familial economic woes are basically due to a relaxing of some doctrinal position of the Witnesses. The alleviation of the condition lies in the fortifying of the faith.

This kind of thinking is no more than the inevitable result of the Witness's craving for completeness. One cannot have an eclectic attitude toward creeds, easily accepting this and absorbing that from other traditions. He cannot believe only as much as reason allows if he expects to remain a Witness. If a Witness is unable to accept a particular belief that the Society cherishes, then he is taken aside by other Witnesses and persuaded that his trouble is that he hasn't really made a complete surrender to Jehovah's will. Sometimes it is suggested that perhaps Satan is gaining on him in the race. They may pray that Satan may be cast out.

The Witness considers that a "doctrine of destiny" has come into his life. This is quite sufficient for his motivation toward hard work, personal sacrifice, and ultimate salvation. He doesn't really need a creed. For the convenience of those who may wish to refresh themselves and understand anew what the correct formula is for obtaining salvation, there is a statement of belief that is published regularly:

THE SCRIPTURES CLEARLY TEACH

That Jehovah is the only true God and is from everlasting to everlasting, the Maker of heaven and earth and the Giver of life to his creatures; that the Logos was the beginning of his creation, and his active agent in the creation of all things, and is now the Lord Jesus Christ in glory, clothed with all power in heaven and earth, as the Chief Executive Officer of Jehovah;

That God created the earth for man, created perfect man for the earth and placed him upon it; that man willfully disobeyed God's law and was sentenced to death; that by reason of Adam's wrong act all men are born sinners and without the right to life;

That the Logos was made human as the man Jesus and suffered death in order to produce the ransom or redemptive price for obedient ones of mankind; that God raised up Jesus divine and exalted him to heaven above every other creature and above every name and clothed him with all power and authority;

That Jehovah's Organization is a Theocracy known as Zion, and that Christ Jesus himself is the Chief Officer thereof and is the rightful King of the world; that the anointed and faithful followers of Christ Jesus are children of Zion, members of Jehovah's organization, and are his witnesses whose duty and privilege it is to testify to the supremacy of Jehovah, declare his purposes toward mankind as expressed in the Bible, and to bear the fruits of the Kingdom before all who will hear;

That the Old World ended in A.D. 1914, and the
Lord Jesus Christ has been placed by Jehovah
upon his throne of authority, has ousted Satan
from heaven and is proceeding to the establishment of the "new earth" of the New World;

That the relief and blessings of the peoples of
the earth can come only by and through
Jehovah's kingdom under Christ, which has now
begun; that the Lord's next great act is the
destruction of Satan's organization and the complete establishment of righteousness in the earth,
and that under the Kingdom the people of good
will that survive Armageddon shall carry out the
divine mandate to "fill the earth" with a
righteous race.

If you fail to discover the real significance of the theology of
the Jehovah's Witnesses, it is because its inner meanings
are open only to true believers. One cannot validate
Witness truth until *after* one has accepted it.

7

Jehovah's Headquarters

As my interest and curiosity in the phenomenon of Jehovah's Witnesses slowly grew, I became vaguely aware that I had noticed a building on the East River waterfront in Brooklyn that had a sort of watchtower cupola on the top with the words "Watchtower Bible and Tract Society" emblazoned on it. I consulted the Brooklyn telephone directory for the specific street address and took the subway to Brooklyn to the Boro Hall station. The half-mile walk provided me with an opportunity to see *all* the buildings of the Society against the background of that part of the city where they have had their headquarters since the days when Pastor Russell acquired the Henry Ward Beecher residence. I was not prepared to see so many buildings that were the property of the Watchtower Bible and Tract Society. To begin with, there were four of them, each taking up a separate small block. They were connected by walkways over the streets at about the fourth floor so that one did not have to go all the way down to the street to cross it and enter another building.

The Manhattan Bridge entrance on the Manhattan side of the East River is a good distance from the Brooklyn Bridge. But on the Brooklyn side of the river, the exit ramps of both bridges are nearly shared. The Society's buildings are set down on the waterfront between and almost among the Medusa-like curving ramps that give entrance and exit to these bridges. The buildings were easy to spot, for they were in the process of being painted a bright but pleasing golden yellow trimmed in bright green, hopefully their last paint job before Armageddon. Against the drab buildings surrounding the Society's properties (mostly warehouses), the color made up somewhat for the plainness of the architecture. These four buildings were warehouse-type buildings and apparently used exclusively for printing the Witness literature.

Walking around this group of buildings, each looking exactly like the other, I finally came to what was a most unpretentious main entrance. Upon entering the building, I came directly into an anteroom which led to a shipping room. I was right in the middle of the operation. It turned out that I wasn't in the lobby of the main office building after all. There was a young man standing at a counter wrapping a small package for the person ahead of me. When my turn came I asked him where I might buy a copy of the Witness songbook. He explained politely to me that there were no songbooks in this building but that he could direct me to the one of these four buildings where there should be some of the books available.

As I walked into the correct entrance, I came into another room exactly like the one in the first building. It could even have been the same young man at the counter. I made the same request and received the same answer. However, this young man withdrew a small printed map of the neighborhood. He explained to me where I was and where I must go from here for the songbook.

I left the warehouse quartet and set off for a ten-minute walk that wound me around the cloverleaf ramps. I came to another cluster of warehouse buildings dressed in golden yellow and green. I entered a third anteroom almost exactly like the first two. Here again there were two customers ahead of me. I noticed that they were both picking up material, apparently for use in their home Kingdom Hall. As I succeeded to the counter, the customer ahead of me turned to leave, giving me a quick glance.

"You aren't one of the brothers, are you?" he asked.

I was somewhat taken aback, thinking in a vague way that he thought he recognized something about me that gave me some kind of religio-fraternal distinction. "Brother?" I answered. "Well, no, but I'm not sure I know what you mean," I explained as I stumbled about trying to understand what he was talking about.

"I meant that I didn't think you were one of us Witnesses," he explained.

"No, I'm not," I said. Then I added, smiling, "I think my little goatee gave me away, didn't it?"

"Well, yes, it did," he confessed. "I was just surprised to run into anybody down here who wasn't one of us, because I hardly ever meet anybody else when I come down to pick up materials."

I went on to explain what I was doing here and that I was not a "spy." He laughed when I said that. "I have become quite interested in the movement," I said. "I came down here to buy a copy of the Witness songbook. Ever since I read that Judge Rutherford said that singing was frivolous and a waste of valuable time, and that several years passed after his death before a songbook was published, I wanted to have one for my own examination." I turned to the beaming young man at the counter who thought that he sensed another prospect in my person. As he passed me the songbook, he was rippling with smiling attention. "Can you tell me where I go to take the subway back to Manhattan?" I asked.

My new friend, thinking by now that perhaps Jehovah had led him to another one of the lost sheep of Israel, quickly offered to escort me there. He explained quickly that he was going past the station on his way to another one of the Society's buildings. I was beginning to think that *all* the buildings on the Brooklyn waterfront were filled with printing presses that belonged to the Jehovah's Witnesses. I accepted his invitation and we began the short walk. "You seem to know your way around here quite well," I said. "Do you come down here often?"

"At least once a week," he said as we trudged up the steep hill at Columbia Drive. "I drive a bus down from upstate New York every day to the Port Authority Building up on Eighth Avenue. Then I have until 4:30 in the afternoon before I make the return trip. So I have a lot of time on my hands. I usually get my reading and studying done. I usually go over and sit in the Reading Room of the New York Public Library where I can spread out my stuff and not be bothered. Today I had to pick up some stuff for our Kingdom Hall. I'm the messenger boy for our fellowship back home," he explained.

"How long have you been a Witness?" I ventured.

"Ever since I gave up drinking, beating my wife, and tom-catting around the countryside. Jehovah God shook me up good about twenty years ago. He told me then and there when I was having one of my hangovers that if I wanted to commit suicide real slow, just keep on the way I'm going and then I'll miss out on some mighty interesting doings that are coming up. Of course, he was telling me about Armageddon, but I didn't know that at the time. My wife says that Jehovah moved right in without a minute to spare when he took hold of me. She said that we were both almost goners, me from my sins and her from my beatings. So my life is full of thanks. I live the Witness life now, and so does my wife. She says that anybody that could do what was done with me should be listened to and obeyed, and here we are. I drive a bus to pay my way through life, that's all. I bet I'll drive this bus right up to Armageddon date. I hope it won't happen when I'm out on the highway, but after I get everybody home. I don't know how I'd hold up if it happened while we were all on the bus. I've gotten to know most of these passengers and they aren't Witnesses and they don't stand a chance of coming through Armageddon. I just don't want to be around when their bodies start falling apart and all that."

"With a spirit like yours, I can easily understand how and why the Society flourishes," I commented as we sauntered along on the downgrade side of the hill. Neither of us was in a great rush.

Coming to the next short rise, we stopped again to catch our breaths. "Armageddon'll be quite a sight from here, won't it?" he speculated. "Just think, all the brothers and sisters working in those buildings will see those Manhattan buildings sway and fall over! Boy! There'll be some excitement all right. But I think I'd just as soon be home."

"Sure will," I agreed, gazing at the financial district skyline across the water to see if I could detect even a slight swaying movement yet. "And like you, I'd rather be somewhere else if and when it happens, such as out in Montana at the time."

He didn't pick up my "if and when" conditional phrase, but went right ahead. "It won't really make that much difference," he said. "Armageddon'll be there too, but you'll have mountains falling on you, as Jesus said in Luke 23:30:

Then they will start to say to the mountains,
Fall over us!" and to the hills. "Cover us over!"

He allowed a brief silence as though waiting for it to sink in. We resumed our walk. He asked me if I had ever been through the printing operations. I told him that I had not done so, but would like to have the opportunity. He said that he could arrange it for me to have a tour of the building where everybody lives and perhaps have lunch there sometime in the near future.

"Anytime before Armageddon," he answered a bit jauntily. "Why don't we set a date for about two weeks? I can meet you where we met a few minutes ago and take you around. It'll be easy to do. I have all day free, as I told you, and I can arrange things because they all know me around here."

We set a date for two weeks hence. Soon after, we came to the subway station. We had a handshake and an exchange of our names and an understanding that we would meet in two weeks at ten in the morning at that same counter. Thanking him for his help and friendship, I went down the subway stairs as he went his way with a smile and a wave of his hand.

8

A Commune for the Lord

The day of the meeting arrived and coincided with the rare occasion when there was no waiting necessary for the subway train. It was one of those days when one could go down the stairs, through the turnstiles, and onto a waiting train. As a result, I showed up ahead of time for my appointment by about ten minutes. Waiting inside the entrance to the building where I had previously met my future guide, I explained my loitering presence to the neatly groomed and rather intent young man standing behind the counter. All four of these buildings, being at the exit ramps of the Manhatten Bridge and only about a block away from the ramps of the Brooklyn Bridge, were extremely noisy and smoggy places. Working in an environment such as this would be bound not only to fortify one's faith constantly by convincing one that the end *must* be at hand, but also to give one a foretaste of the overture to Armageddon. The din outside was maddening.

In due time my guide arrived and met his prospect (me). A chapter-and-verse recital of the tour is unnecessary, I think; suffice it to say that the sheer magnitude of the printing and publishing operation of the Watchtower Bible and Tract Society is most impressive. There is no loitering around the water coolers here. There are no clusters of workers wasting Jehovah's time in standing around the entrance doorways during work breaks—if indeed there are such events. Everyone is busy at his job producing warnings of the nearness of the last days. There is a distinct "work-for-the-night-is-coming" flavor and aura to this publishing hive. It is hard to realize that when the Society publishes anything from a book to the next issue of *Watchtower* or *Awake!* they are not printing in modest numbers, as most of the 36,000 books that are printed annually by the American publishing industry are. The figures are high in the thousands here. There is no way of knowing how their output compares with other publishing companies and printing houses, but the Witnesses appear to be ahead of whoever is in second place.

The people employed in this operation receive the same pay as everybody else—maintenance personnel, housekeeping, and so on, up to and including the administrative officers and the president. There are no exceptions. It is the same for everybody, except of course, for those persons who work part-time while they are receiving their Gilead training for overseas full-time work.

By my count the Witnesses' base of operations here in Brooklyn is spread out over ten buildings. No modest operation here. Each of these buildings is of considerable size, each five to ten stories tall. Six of these buildings are given over to printing and shipping. The other four are used for the living arrangements of both the workers and the students. The kind of inquiry that I would like to make of such an enterprise as this is exceedingly difficult to ac-

complish, because such an effort is indirectly and politely
discouraged. As a result, it takes twice as long to discover
the needed facts. There is no conspiracy of silence here.
But one definitely feels oneself to be outside of things, and
that one is being casually observed by members of a benign
secret society. This was in all likelihood due to the intensity of dedication toward getting the work done before the
call to arms and Armageddon. The climate of urgency
permeates the whole atmosphere here.

The part of the total enterprise that I was most interested in seeing was the administrative arm and the living arrangements. Making our way around and through the
serpentine ramps of the bridges, we came out the other end
into a quiet neighborhood of tree-lined streets, a remnant
of old Brooklyn of another generation. Old two- and three-
story brownstone apartments lined the narrow streets. The
Witness buildings, all named Bethel, face on Willow
Street. On the west side of the street, the oldest of these
buildings abruptly abuts the Brooklyn-Queens Ex-
pressway, which runs directly beneath the awninged extension of a walkway facing the East River. On the other side
of that speedway are docked ocean-going freighters from all
around the world. Directly across the East River at this
point looms the financial district of Wall Street and lower
Manhattan Island dominated by the twin towers of the
World Trade Mart. What a front-row seat for Armageddon
this site would be!

The largest of the brick buildings is on the former site of
the manse of Henry Ward Beecher on Columbia Heights,
whose Plymouth Church of the Pilgrims is but a short
block away on Orange Street. Although these modern
buildings are conservative and utilitarian in appearance,
they are not severe, but are actually attractive and fit into
the neighborhood inobtrusively. There is no Babylon here.
That begins on the other side of the ramp, where the print-

ing factory works in the midst of Satan's world. The temperature this day was in the nineties. All doors and windows were opened wide. The absence of air-conditioning under such conditions can bring one's mind back to the urgency of the last days.

Directly across the street from the first Bethel is a building whose cornerstone announces that its birthdate was in the year 1959. The entrance was set back from the street so that one had to stroll down a lengthy court to get to it. There were shade trees here and a profusion of roses of all kinds within squares bordered with verbena and salvia. The small plats of grass had been so painstakingly groomed and manicured that the blades stood apart from each other in a serried sameness, all alike in height, texture, and health. It struck me at that moment that possibly each blade of grass had been personally seeded, cultivated, and possibly transplanted. The uniformity exceeded that of Astro-turf and was obviously real in spite of what might have been taken for a homogenized production. I suppressed the vagrant speculation as to what the gardeners would have done if they had been placed in charge of setting and placing the stars. Surely they would have been in rows, and equally bright and twinkly. There were two young men there who were fussing over the roses that did not need anything done for them, although I think that I detected the roses enjoying the magic feeling of touch.

The roses and the grass resembled the earnest and intent young men who were manning the desks wherever I went on my tour. As my guide and I were invited by the color and quietness of this garden to sit down and enjoy, one of the gardeners turned on a small water fountain. We sat there listening, watching, and absorbing the scene, soaking up the climate of this probable sample of the soon-to-come new Eden. In a way, it was an advance sign of their expectancies. There were not even any insects buzzing around.

This was the most beautifully and exactingly planned, cultivated, and sanitized court garden that I have ever seen. The love and care—compulsive and obsessive though it may have been—made the court a place where one stopped for a moment to let his soul catch up with his body as he sat down and considered the lilies of the field and Solomon and all his glory.

The double glass entrance doors were open and beckoning. In we went, facing the welcoming sign on the opposite panelled wall:

WALKING IN THE NAME OF JEHOVAH—AROUND THE WORLD

The message was in raised letters. Around and below the pronouncement were large colored pictures of some of their Kingdom Halls in Greenland, Fiji, Austria, Africa, and Pakistan. "From Greenland's icy mountains to India's coral strand" came to mind. This early 19th-century hymn of the Anglican Church has been out of style for at least two generations in that body, but its spirit lives on among the Witnesses:

Can we whose souls are lighted with wisdom from on high?
Can we to men benighted the lamp of life deny?
From many an ancient river, from many a palmy plain,
They call us to deliver their land from error's chain.

A strange ironic twist, that these lines were composed by a Church of England missionary bishop in India back in 1817!

Nothing fancy in any of these buildings. True to Witness convictions, they are meant to last only until Armageddon. Hence, no extras. The rooms, lounges and dining halls are institutional and utilitarian. They are even more spotlessly maintained than the court garden, if this be possible. Even more shiny than a modern hospital corridor. The attitude of the Witnesses is one of taking these things as they are and looking ahead to the new Eden, rather than dressing up the tired old world of Satan.

Everyone who works here—in the offices, the factory, or the shipping buildings—lives here. They have their own laundry, dry-cleaning plant, and complete maintenance shops, including shoe repair. This latter must certainly be a busy place, what with all the pavement pounding that goes on and all the mileage racked up by the publishers and the trainees. As I was about to find out, they raise almost all their own food. They used to have a large farm near Ithaca, New York, at a place called South Lansing. Here, too, was the Gilead School to train workers for the overseas mission fields. This project has been transferred to Brooklyn. Being ever practical-minded stewards of Jehovah, they discovered that students could be put to better use in the printing and shipping aspects of the work than they could as farm hands in upstate New York. Their growing need for more help in the publishing department almost necessitated the change. The students were also available for training in house-to-house calling in metropolitan areas—always the hardest to do. This also gave them the opportunity to develop skills in conducting the Bible study classes, too. Now the farms—presently about 1,400 acres of land between Newburgh and New Paltz, New York, as well as one in northern New Jersey—raise their own Angus, Charolais, and Hereford cattle as well as all other livestock, poultry, and dairy products for the use of the Brooklyn Bethel. The original farm and school at South Lansing were sold to the State of New York and are now being used as a treatment center for disturbed children.

There are many kinds of communes, or communities, that have come into existence today to serve the needs of every conceivable purpose. The Jehovah's Witnesses have been running a very large community for years long before it became the thing to do. Most of the newer communities are characterized by an attempt to return to the simpler life. They are typified by succeeding in a large degree to keep free from the entanglements of a culture that seems to community members to be more and more self-destructive, and of a society that is systematically poisoning itself through its technology, including the preparation and processing of its foods.

The Witnesses are old hands at community life. The Watchtower Bible School of Gilead was such an establishment in its earlier days. Its present form is simply a more practical and sophisticated operation in the heart of the city. At one time, those being trained for full-time ministries shared in the raising of the food. But now at Bethel they are right in the middle of the excitement of the last days at the home office.

Visiting here at Bethel, one is reminded constantly that everybody here is a minister, but not in the conventional sense of the Christian sectarian meaning. By their very membership and presence here, they are ministers—not only working, but learning how to do their job better.

The school here is made up of Witnesses who, after working for the call they have dreamed of receiving, are at long last being prepared by the Society to fulfill their personal visions. The "call" of these students is to serve the Society in a full-time ministry in a foreign land, a country in which no one has a selective choice, but to which you are appointed, or better yet, "sent." You are likely to spend the rest of your life there "singing the Lord's song in a strange land," as the Psalmist sings.

A person who eventually becomes a student here does not decide exclusively on his own whether or not this is what he would like to do for his life's work—or at least up until Armageddon. First, he is required to have had considerable experience of a faithful, full-time ministry either in the United States or some foreign country. You are "called" up, not "volunteered" up. You don't pick them. They pick you.

You must first have a certain minimal educational background. Your temperament and personality structure (although they would not use the phrase) must fit in with what the powers-that-be regard as indispensable for a successful ministry in overseas situations. Those who come here from other countries must have a good working knowledge of the English language, because they are going to spend much time in digging around in the Scriptures in English in the development and training that they will be receiving in "biblical theology."

They come from all over the world and demonstrate that the human family is basically one family. These people live like it here at the world headquarters in Brooklyn. All nationalities and cultures blend together and become indistinguishable. The graduates of the school are trained in how to go out into the world and teach others how to bring the countries together permanently. Those of each country who have come here will return to the service and dedication of their lives to Jehovah God for the duration. When the imminent end finally arrives, then they may have eternal life upon earth along with those whom they have guided into their path of eternal salvation.

They are graded on all aspects of their work, including their work in the printing factory operation. Their training is designed to enlighten, mature, and unite the cream of Witness missionaries, who are in turn sent out to bring together the peoples of the nations in the permanent New World Society that is preparing Jehovah's people for the day of Armageddon.

The thoroughness of their instruction is impressive. These students have been uprooted from their home cir-

cumstances and environment and placed in a totally new
and strange situation in a big city. They are outsiders un-
acquainted with anybody prior to their arrival here. Their
life is tightly organized without explanation. Everyone
may safely assume that it is all part of the Witness
program to prepare and produce effective and competent
missionaries. The student is loaded to the maximum with
classes, study time, and work time in an environment that
is highly stimulative. It is a six-month cram course in
which the fatigue level is maintained carefully just below
collapse, but high enough to keep resistance and rejection
of Witness ideas that may be new to the student from
entering into the picture. It is a highly developed and refined
bit of "thought-reform" directed toward good ends.
Moreover, the individual is never quite sure of just where
he stands in the opinion of his superiors. Approval is the
carrot in front of the horse. He is encouraged to keep striv-
ing and "everything will soon fit together for you." The
final step, at the end of the training period and the school
term, is the "tail-cutting" operation. This is not even a rite
or a ceremony. It is nothing more than the reaching of that
point in the individual's life where the point of no return
has been reached. From here on one belongs to Jehovah,
and is sent by Him, through the student's superiors, to
where he may best use his talents, gifts, and training to
warn the most people to return to the Lord before the Day
of Wrath.

The student knows beforehand that if he survives the
training—which is likely because of the selective
process—when he graduates he will receive his assignment.
During the bulk of his time spent at Gilead, he will not
have the remotest idea of where he will be sent. He regards
himself somewhat like a diplomatic service graduate. He
stays where he is sent, until otherwise notified. This might
well last until Armageddon, although there is always the

chance that he may be recalled and sent to another field where his peculiar and special abilities may be more critically needed. Every student looks upon himself as an expensive investment of the Society. After all, it was the Society that paid the student's way to the States and is supporting him while he is here. His way will also be paid to whatever country he has been assigned. He would be looked after wherever he went. He would receive no salary, wages, or stipend, but "he would be taken care of." Their part of the bargain was to cooperate with the program while in training. They know that they are here to work and learn so that they may be able to preach and teach better and to serve as the theocratic example in that part of the world in which Jehovah God, through His Witnesses, was pleased to send them.

"Take your assignment as though it were from Jehovah," the student is counselled. They are not made to feel that they may be going to a foreign country, but to a *new home*. As Abraham of old was called by Jehovah from his native land into a "foreign assignment," you may be surrounded by enemy people where you are sent. It is made honestly and clearly right from the first that you may stay on your first assignment until death or Armageddon. This is not to be regarded as failure to advance, but success by faithfulness in what one is doing where he is. "Carry out your assignment in love, even as father Abraham. You will find out quickly that love for new-found persons removes all strangeness so that you will not feel like an alien among them for very long."

This school, along with its whole philosophy and structure, has clearly demonstrated throughout its whole life that there *is* a way wherein men of all nations may be drawn together when they can live, learn, and work together in unity, happiness, and a profound sense of accomplishing something that is lasting and so very worthwhile. By the time a Gilead student has completed his training, he could be sent anywhere in the world, regardless of his nationality or cultural background. There he would raise his family, and perhaps spend a lifetime among his adopted people.

Care is also used to see to it that an elite is not built up. It soon becomes clear to everybody that the difference is slight between the overseas missionary and the Witness who serves in a local field ministry part-time while holding a secular job to meet his expenses of life, raising his family, and maintaining a necessary position of permanency in his community. For the person who does not have a long-term family commitment, or a life situation where he is "locked in," he too has a vital role in the life of the Society exactly where he is living.

Full-time Witnesses and part-time Witnesses share one viewpoint about the organization. They see the scene as one great family with Jehovah God as father, and everyone else as brothers and sisters. At home base everyone should come to Kingdom Hall meetings prepared to meet any emergency. Everyone is expected to bring others, to make them feel welcome, to volunteer services, to keep confidence with the organization, and to be content with an enlightened conscience. Whether in school as the guest and candidate of the Society, or on your home ground, certain things are expected of you. All excuses are made to sound weak and invalid.

The student is given a fuller understanding of the role of the part-time minister. He is made to realize how important he is in his present place. He is shown how he is supposed to be the one who knows his way around a community and "how to get things done." Wherever he goes he is likely to become a taxpayer and a property holder. Because of these probabilities he will have a built-in way of receiving community trust and understanding. His neighbors will find him outwardly enmeshed in a pagan and secular society because of these things, just as they are, too.

It is here at the school that the student is at once taught how to schedule and use his time, how to divide and allot it for study, for work, for meeting and for other service. He is shown how to fit a schedule into the life pattern that will be absolutely necessary wherever he is going to live and carry on Jehovah's work. He is cautioned against over-planning and having too tight a schedule. He is helped to avoid the subtle pitfall of squandered time. This is regarded as the most valuable resource to a Witness, especially the missionary. From the head office down to the teaching staff at Gilead, they are aware that time is coming in shorter and shorter supply these days. It is indeed another sign of the approach of the end, like everything else in our contemporary society. The student is impressed with the feeling that only a thimbleful of time remains, so it is of utmost importance that it be used to the best advantage. These trained workers help congregation workers see their mistakes. They set the better way before them and help them to become oriented into a new theocratic life pattern from which everyone benefits. Health is also stressed, along with its preservation and proper use, although the Society has none of the dietary laws that are fairly common in millennial groups.

The worker is trained to help the part-time minister discover his own hidden talents and resources so that he will have an advantage when he goes out into the world on his own as a responsible Witness answerable to the home office. The staff members all help him to develop, refine, and dedicate his special abilities through cultivation and proper study, that the individual may be more balanced in Jehovah. They try at all times to help him realize what an influence he is in the community. The student is shown how he can help the part-time ministers who will be under him to understand that there are several things they will be able to do in a community better and with greater ease than the full-time missionary.

The full-time minister-in-training is helped to show the future congregation minister that everything in his life must be built around dedication to Jehovah. There must be order and harmony in his home. His house and yard must be well-kept as an example to the neighborhood and pride in their own Jehovah God. The children of the Witnesses must be exemplary in conduct, for they are being watched and judged by the outsider. Social life must be restricted primarily to Witness associates. He is expected to work hard, conscientiously and devotedly, not like most men on a daily job. He knows what Jehovah expects of him and he does it. "Awaken the brothers to their advantages. Show them how to overcome their weaknesses. Always be cheerful and positive. Support them in their lives and they will support you in yours. You owe these things to the Society and to Jehovah."

The Witness student is also given an extensive and intensive course in public speaking. This is not done in order to transform him into a spellbinding platform speaker. It is done to give poise, self-assurance, and articulation to a person who is going forth into the world as a leader of men to draw others to the dedication of their lives to Jehovah. This is obviously much harder to do if one has not developed his abilities at speaking, for this is the greatest single aid that there is that can help one arouse the curiosity and self-interest of the hearer. As a result, the principles of public speaking learned here are used as examples and standards by thousands of people throughout more than 160 countries around the world. Through this school they have developed the kind of instruction that is carried on in their congregational training schools that are in operation in local Kingdom Halls throughout the country. It has given to Jehovah's Witnesses the largest body of poised, capable, and regularly performing speakers that will be found anywhere. No other society can make that statement.

Besides the courses in what are called "Missionary Service" and public speaking, the students are also given intensive drills in "Scripture Fact." The overall attempt here is to help the student see the whole scriptural picture and to help him focus the world-scene into a three-dimensional diorama, in a sense. It is carefully explained that the theologians are quite mistaken when they teach that although man is a defective species and hence the world is insane, yet beneath it all there is an evolution of the spirit that slowly guides the doings of men. The Witness will have nothing whatever to do with that kind of reasoning. Contrarily, they show, at least to their own satisfaction, that nothing but total and complete destruction and a complete starting over again will make any difference to mankind.

The view of history is necessarily somewhat constricted, because it also follows the history of nations as recorded in the Bible. One can only presume that nations and cultures not mentioned here were not regarded as factors in the knit garment of history, the divine shawl revealing the tapestry of man and his doings down through the years. The one exception to all this is the acceptance of the presence of the modern state as revealed in the British and American Empires. Present-day communist states are apparently regarded as even more fleeting and ephemeral, not having lived long enough to be regarded as major civilizations with their threads woven into the scenes of history.

By stretching a definition, one might possibly call the fourth course "Biblical Theology," although the study is mostly confined to interpretations of Scripture that help guide a person in his personal life. For example, a chapter from the New Testament is read in class and talked over. The course is a word-by-word investigation of the "Christian Greek Scriptures," as the Witnesses prefer to call the New Testament. But it is done in English according to their *New World Translation* with the assistance of *The Kingdom Interlinear Translation of the Greek Scriptures*, which is based on the scholarly work of the nineteenth-century English scholars Westcott and Hort. The passages are read and explained. They are then applied to daily life and conduct.

The classroom work at the school is designed to give to the student all that he can hold of knowledge that is required by Jehovah to live in the Edenic world-soon-to-come. The community life is carried out in such a way that the student may learn first-hand how to model theocratic community lives. The printing factory, the shipping room, the classroom, and the daily routine of the community are all one, and hang together in cadence. It is designed so that the student learns equally from each one of the sides and aspects of their common life together. Also, each student, as well as the staff, teach and learn, live and work as though this might be the last class to go through training. They are certain that there will not be very many more.

The weekends for the student are filled with field preaching. This means going out into the surrounding communities and distributing copies of *The Watchtower* and *Awake!*, the two magazines of the Society. There is also Saturday classwork as well as field work. In the main, this consists of going over the material and experiences of the past week and fitting them all together. It is a weekend "assimilation period." The flow and input of information and know-how has been intensive. He has been trying all week to cope with the torrent of information that has been drenching him. Now he tries to sort it out and put it into an emerging order. He has the help of instructors in this process, thankfully. The learning experience may be compared somewhat to a weekly swim across a wide river. Saturday is the day the student surfaces from the flowing river of information and knowledge that he has probably been thrashing around in. Now he takes a look back at where he has been and how far he has come—and how distant the other shore still is. Each week is a leg of a six-month relay race. With these weekly flashbacks it has been found that the student finds it easier to keep up with the organizing and assimilating of all the new and voluminous content with which he has been grappling during the previous five days. Now for a change of pace. But there is no real let-up in the learning experience. The process of thought-reform goes on its relentless path.

Instructors, students, and the farm families live in close quarters. They have the same kind of living arrangements. There are no grades of difference. The accommodations are adequate and comfortable. They are probably a lot better than they would find in their native lands. They are plain. They are large enough for two people. The furniture in one room is the same as that in another, like a military academy. The only differences are what the students, instructors, and other personnel bring in of their own property, such as radio and television sets and personal accoutrements.

The instructors, as well as the office, publishing, and maintenance personnel have been brought here out of the various phases of the work of the Society. They are obviously dedicated people to live in such close quarters, share common meals and have intertwined lives for extended periods of time. It is much like attending a prolonged and seemingly endless church camp or conference. There is no let-up. Husbands and wives share a room. It is their only privacy. The life here is entirely and totally institutional, and includes everybody, just like a conference or a camp. There are no exceptions due to rank. They have discovered through this common life that they have a common denominator for peace, harmony, and unity as children of Jehovah as they prepare for the creation of the New Eden.

They have managed to integrate the different racial and national backgrounds of both staff and students and the young and the old. Everyone, regardless of his place in the structure, has the same degree of interest in the life and welfare. Discipline is practically nonexistent. First of all, the guest-students are carefully screened. There isn't anybody here who isn't interested in everything that is going on and that the Society believes in and stands for. Not only do they bring their enthusiasm into the school but they take it with them when they leave. They extend the Gilead spirit into every area that it has pleased Jehovah to send them. They transfer their fire and love to whatever congregation and fellowship they may be appointed to lead. This is all the more admirable when one considers that this happy condition simply does not exist in any other school of any religious body that trains young and old for service in the field. The Witnesses alone have made it work, largely because of their sense of urgency about the whole matter that sets them apart among people. What can one do but have admiration for them and what they are accomplishing, whether you can accept their ideas and beliefs or not?

9

Householders for Jehovah

Almost everyone is acquainted with the plainly attractive brick building of modified colonial design that announces to all who pass by that this is a Kingdom Hall of the Jehovah's Witnesses. One of these small, well-kept buildings may be found in nearly every village, town, or city in the country. The grounds are spacious and manicured. Almost every night of the week the parking lot is likely to be filled with automobiles. The utilitarian building is alive with meetings of various kinds. One cannot help but compare the extensive and continuous use of this modest building with those large parish halls built of stone, glass, and aluminum that are used to their full capacity no more than three hours a week at the most. It horrifies a Witness to know that so much capital is tied up in a property for religious purposes that is being used so minimally. Not so with the Witnesses. They get mileage out of their properties. Everything that is going on there is directed toward the preparation of the Witnesses for the great day of Armageddon and for spreading the word among the people of the community that this building is in happy and anticipatory use and that the Witnesses are busy about Jehovah's work. It *is* something of a rebuke to modern, conventionalized culture-churches who never seem to be busy promoting and professing their faith.

It was not always this way with the Witnesses. These neat and attractive properties are comparatively new. The meeting places in the old days used to be rented halls, store fronts, and tacky suites of rooms in deteriorating buildings whose only virtue was low rent. In some areas in the larger cities, these conditions still prevail, especially in the ghettos of various ethnic groups. These places that remind one of the Kingdom Halls of other days are largely headquarters for front-line offensives in city neighborhoods that are deteriorating even more rapidly than the buildings, and where there is little or no choice for the Witnesses to make in selecting their local Kingdom Hall. Elsewhere their pleasant and utilitarian halls have become easy to spot.

A Kingdom Hall is not looked upon as the House of God so much as it is a learning center where everyone—oldtimer and recent convert—as well as those in the process of becoming Witnesses, can meet together to learn how to spread the word as well as to fortify one another's faith. The Society loudly and emphatically condemns the building of cathedrals and large churches, believing that such buildings do not get the job done for God. They are regarded, and not without some justification, as eventual liabilities because of costly maintenance and the tying up of huge amounts of capital and the straining of a budget to maintain such properties. It is noteworthy that when a congregation grows too large for a Kingdom Hall to accommodate the group, they do not add to the building in any way. A new congregation is started elsewhere and another building of like size and design is immediately built. Most of the cost and labor are borne by the local fellowship themselves. When the subject is mentioned the Witness forthrightly informs you that neither the individual Witness, nor the Society itself, for that matter, is interested in tying up capital and paying out interest to maintain an impressive architectural layout for their own ego satisfactions for a God whom the Witnesses know is indifferent to such show. The Witnesses are also aware that there isn't one of these fine buildings that can possibly survive the divine wrath at Armageddon.

In plain words, Kingdom Hall is a meeting place for the Witnesses to gather for more and more Bible instruction and further constant training in their publishing ministry. The Witnesses have become known as "publishers of glad tidings, the justice of Jehovah." The term does not mean the printing of books in this case but the spreading of the news of the Last Days. Therefore, all Witnesses, being ministers of Jehovah through baptism, *are* clergymen technically when they are engaged in their house-to-house ministry.

It is here that the publisher comes to report the results of his work each week. This is where he goes to receive his supply of literature, to keep abreast of what is going on in the Society both here and elsewhere. This is the place where the latest plans and strategies are presented to him as they come forth from Bethel House in Brooklyn. Kingdom Hall is also the place where they will be married and buried, in their fashion. This building is for them the center of their social and spiritual lives. The Witnesses reject all local community organizations as futile because their energies are not directed toward the end of things and the rolling up of the scroll of time. These small buildings, and the life within, are the very center of their lives. Their friends are all here. This is the one place where those who have withdrawn from the secular world may meet together in harmony, peace, and unity of purpose. It is here that the publisher will eventually bring his prospect when the time is right so that his curiosity (and his self-interest) may be further aroused, that he may receive a picture of the organization and experience the size, power, and wisdom of the movement. However, this is a much later follow-up of the initial house call made weeks beforehand, and after there have been several weekly home Bible study meetings with the prospect.

The main missionary thrust of the Jehovah's Witnesses is this weekly home Bible study. It is through these contacts, originally made through their endless house-to-house canvassing, that it is possible for the publisher to establish a beachhead in a particular home. The attempt is made to help the person commit himself to an hour a week of Bible study with the publisher—and a colleague, usually a learner or beginner at this business, for this is how he learns.

By this suggestion for a home Bible study plan, the curious person and prospect imagines that he is being asked to join with them in a free discussion of the Bible. This is not exactly what the publisher had in mind when he stood cheerfully before you at the open door. The idea behind it is to tie one down to a systematic study of Witness teachings in which the Bible is used to substantiate the views that the Society believes. The publisher has become quite skilled through the special training that he has been given so painstakingly at his local Kingdom Hall. He wishes for the prospect to "invite" him *into* the house. A time is then set for the meeting in that home the following week. As this initial first "interview" is concluded, the prospect will not only have in his hand the latest copies of

The Watchtower and *Awake!* magazines, but also probably a booklet that introduces one of the more immediately digestible teachings of the Society.

The prospect will probably have read at least enough of this first booklet to raise some questions for their first meeting. This invariably happens—and usually by deliberate design—because the teachings of the Witnesses are quite likely to be in direct opposition to any orthodox teachings that the prospect is likely either to believe in or to have embraced in times past.

These home meetings are the necessary remote preparation for the day when the prospect is ready to be introduced to the members of the fellowship. They set the stage for his first open meeting and discussion. The home Bible study continues for awhile. The publisher himself is well trained and counseled to play along with this for a few weeks. Then he points out that religion is indeed a large subject and that this kind of discussion can go on indefinitely without leading anywhere or settling anything. He agrees that it may possibly be enlightening and stimulating, but it won't accomplish much in the long run.

When the publisher senses that the prospect is ready to go on from here, he brings forth a book on whatever is being used this season as an opener and primer of study and a guide to Bible discussion. The "course" usually begins with such subjects as "Who is God?"; "Jehovah?"; "Who was Jesus Christ?"; and so on, through the whole range of doctrine from the general to the specific. All of this is, of course, within the Jehovah's Witness context.

The method that is used for Bible study is one of question and answer. In the books the paragraphs are numbered. At the foot of each page there is a corresponding numbered question. Each paragraph has Scripture quotes to back up the statement. The prospect has all this explained to him so that each point may be fully discussed, worked out and understood.

At first this seems to the prospect to be such a reasonable approach that he will usually go along with it. The publisher is counting on the probability that his prospect has a limited knowledge of Scripture. This means nearly anyone but another Witness, as the publisher knows. In most cases the publisher is correct and finds that his suggestions to the prospect are acceptable.

The immediate effect is the change in the center of the stage from prospect to publisher. This gives the Witness a real advantage, this bringing forth of a study guide. From here on the Witness calls the shots. He is now the one who determines what subjects will be discussed, and in what order. He has the added advantage of never having to explain the agenda to the prospect. The publisher is now in charge of the situation. Everybody can sit back and let nature take its course. The first set of rapids has been successfully run. The well-trained and coached Witness follows this pattern of leading his prospect into a descending and tightening spiral of inquiry into the Jehovah Witness interpretation of Holy Scripture. There is no conscious or deliberate attempt to *dupe* the prospect. The Witnesses regard their approach as a practical strategy designed to bring the prospect to a right mind.

The now-interested and still unsuspecting prospect may be allowed to swing in the breeze for two or three meetings while he is quietly and patiently allowed to express his own views and give his own answers. The lack of response and enthusiasm with which his views are received end up with the sinking of the prospect, ideas and all, being submerged with the publisher's gentle and persistent shifting of emphasis over to the study of the Witness book in place of the study of Scripture. The isolated verses from Scripture that have been extracted to suit the Witness's body of faith is now placed before the prospect for consideration. His thoughts are now being replaced by the Witness's thoughts, as contained in whatever book the Witness has brought from headquarters. As one goes further and further into this pattern, a prospect gradually loses the distinctness and personal flavor of his own thought and belief. This method is an exceedingly well-thought-out kind of thought-reform. It works well on any and all who allow themselves a long enough period, or a sufficient number of home sessions of "Bible Study," with the gradual shifting of emphasis and content over to the teachings of the Witnesses' "party-line."

One soon discovers that among the Jehovah's Witnesses there is an impressive unanimity of belief, thought, action, and reaction. No matter what the issue in life may be, one can almost determine what the reaction to it is going to be on the part of the Witness. He easily becomes a theological automat, serving up Scriptural sandwiches or pie according to the button punched. If one asks for an opinion on a subject from a number of different Witnesses, even at different times and places, you can be fairly certain that you will get the same answer. One quickly perceives that the Witness is not really expressing his own considered and thought-out opinion. This has been abandoned long beforehand, discarded in favor of the opinions that the individual Witness has come to believe are the actual thoughts of Jehovah God.

This type of thought control and conformity of both thought and action is a main trait of the Society. This shows up glaringly in the home Bible study method. Believing that every word of the Bible is absolutely and literally true, and that equal weight can be placed on each and every word, they can naturally ignore the literary and historical context of the verses they choose to demonstrate the truth of their beliefs. It does not strike them as a non-sequitur way of study, this skipping from a single verse in Ezekiel to an isolated verse lifted out of Revelation and putting them together even though these books were written five hundred years apart in separate ages and cultures. They regard Jehovah as being above human limitations; therefore, the things he wrote must be regarded the same way: true no matter where, when, or how he said them. To the Witness it does not matter a particle when the different books were written, nor in what original language, style, or cultural background. Jehovah dictated all the books, therefore the Bible is the literal word of God. While these ignored considerations may be important among the writings of men, they are emphatically *not* important in the writings of Jehovah.

Every text has equal value in the Bible, in the understanding of the Witness. The practice they use may be compared somewhat to the placing of thousands of individual pieces of a huge jigsaw puzzle on a large table. Each piece represents a verse from Scripture. The Witness selects from these myriad pieces those he can somehow fit into an intelligible series that will present the kind of picture he is looking for. The picture he comes up with may not give even a portion of the total and true picture that would be gained by using all the pieces. With each verse being equal, and so regarded by the Witness, his mainspring becomes his weakness.

When they say that "the Word of God shall stand forever," and that "Jesus Christ is the same yesterday, today, and forever," there is hardly a quarrel regardless of which brand of orthodoxy is making the judgment on the truth. But when one regards what Moses said to the children of Israel on the eve of the crossing of the Red Sea being said to us today, and applying in the same context, then one comes to a parting of the ways. Or, taking the above verse from the Epistle to the Hebrews, "Jesus Christ is the same yesterday, today, and forever," and reminding the Witness that they teach that Jesus *acquired* divinity and kingship and that he was originally an archangel, thus not always the same, will get one exactly nowhere.

It is out of such reasonings that the Witnesses develop their arguments against blood transfusions. The grounds for rejecting this present-day means of saving life is based on a passage in Genesis and another one in Leviticus:

> Only flesh with its soil—its blood—you must not eat. And, besides that, your blood of your souls shall I ask back.
>
> —Genesis 9:4-5, NWT

> And you must not eat any blood in any places where you dwell, whether that of fowl or that of beast. Any soul who eats any blood, that soul must be cut off from his people.
>
> —Leviticus 7:26, NWT

The use of isolated texts from Scripture is not large, but it is a springboard for diving into doctrine. Although it would take considerable time in reading and research to discover the total number of specific texts that the Witnesses use to support their beliefs, they would boil down to a few that are used over and over again. There are three, however, that one comes across most often:

And just a little while longer, and the wicked one will be no
    more;
And you will certainly give attention to his place, and he
    will not be.
But the meek ones themselves will possess the earth,
And they will indeed find their exquisite delight in the
    abundance of peace.

—Psalm 37:10-11, NWT

According as you have given him authority over all flesh, that, as regards the whole number whom you have given him, he may give them everlasting life. This means everlasting life, their taking in knowledge of you, the only true God, and the one whom you sent forth, Jesus Christ.

—John 17:2-3, NWT

And I saw a new heaven and a new earth; for the former heaven and the former earth had passed away, and the sea is no more . . . With that I heard a loud voice from the throne say: "Look! The tent of God is with mankind, and he will reside with them, and they will be his peoples. And God himself will be with them. And he will wipe out every tear from their eyes, and death will be no more, neither will mourning nor outcry nor pain be any more. The former things have passed away."

—Revelation 21:1-4, NWT

Add to these spot passages the "Little Apocalypse" found in Luke 21:6-33 and Matthew 24:4-42. Serve up a dessert course made up of Revelation, chapters 5 and 6 with a dash of Daniel and you have the foundation of Witness belief.

These are the texts that the prospect will have been introduced to, and whose further study in them will continue after he has been brought to Kingdom Hall meetings. He does not yet realize the commitments that lie ahead for him to make. In the old saw, "procrastination is the thief of time," the Witnesses can be regarded as thieves of time themselves but without any procrastination. They regard this very special kind of thievery as simply putting a person's allotted time on earth to a better use than he could possibly make outside the Society. Sooner or later the time of the devotee will be filled, except for the time that he spends making a living and keeping his family intact. This latter frequently produces pain, for the whole family may not be as dedicated to the Watchtower cause as the head of the house, or the wife, as the case may be. The cost of surviving Armageddon is a life without any spare time for anything, even a time of quiet for oneself. This puts a great strain on the family tie unless both parties share this belief. Even then the sacrifices that they must make are great. Admittedly they are beyond what most of us could either desire or accomplish without that tremendous motivation of the closeness of the end of time that consumes them.

The Society does insist that in divided homes, the believer should be considerate of the unbelievers and share his time with them and thus fulfill his family obligations. Even so, his time will have to be given over increasingly to Jehovah and his organization, the Witnesses. In this atmosphere the unbeliever is made to feel that things will never be the same until the whole family is in this enterprise together. These are some of the things that the prospect has no way of knowing he will have to face in the days immediately ahead. Witnesses quote a passage in Matthew:

> For I came to cause division, with a man against his father, and a daughter against her mother, and a young wife against her mother-in-law. Indeed, a man's enemies will be persons of his own household.
>
> —Matthew 10:35-36, NWT

To the Witness, this is simply a sign of the last days. It may be regrettable, but that's the way it is. The only way to please God, declares the Witness, is to fill every moment of one's time that can be given over to Kingdom activity. This is the final step that a prospect must take. He must also make a public declaration of his dedication by submitting to baptism by immersion. (There are no baptismal tanks in Kingdom Halls, but local indoor pools are often rented for the happy occasion.) Previous baptisms, either by pouring or immersion, don't count. They are regarded as invalid.

At his baptism he vows to give *all* his time and energy to the service of the Kingdom, except of course, the time spent in making a living and fulfilling one's family and parental role. It is explained that a generous Jehovah gives back to each person what time he needs for other things, *after* the total time and life have been surrendered to him. In this way all one's spare time is used for the extension of the Kingdom and the warning of the people of the imminence of Armageddon. He is required sooner or later to fit into his life *all* the duties of those who have been called out from a dying world. The nearness of Armageddon rules out the necessity of so many things, such as education, community projects, and any other long-range plans that one may have for oneself and one's family. Eventually, this means giving over one's vacation time exclusively to the work of Jehovah's Witnesses. The guilt generated by touring the country during a holiday is eventually too heavy. About the only kind of travel and change of scene that becomes available is attending one of the Jehovah's Witnesses conventions—gloriously exciting times.

And at the convention that took place shortly before the death of Judge Rutherford, he orated:

> If this be the last convention to be held by God's faithful people prior to Armageddon, then we will look forward with unabated joy to that great and glorious convention that shall never end.

Now, once more for the moment, back to the prospect. He has extended the hospitality of his home several times to the Witnesses who have met weekly with him. They have shared their scriptural knowledge and Witness interpretations with him. They have tried to express their understanding and convictions of the truths of Scripture, especially those passages that have been laterally excised. The prospect finds it easier and easier to make these quantum leaps of interpretation. The time comes for him when his sense of proportion and judgement is no longer disturbed. The next move is to be introduced to the fellowship at Kingdom Hall.

10

"The Good News of the Kingdom Let Us Preach!"

Now that a number of weeks have gone by and weekly appointments for Bible study have been going on, let us return to our householder, knowing a little bit in advance of what is about to happen to him. The publisher now feels that the time is ripe and right. The prospect is at last considered to be at the proper stage of development. He is about to be invited to go to Kingdom Hall.

His preparation for this has been going on for quite awhile. Lately, the last few minutes of each Bible study class have been more and more directed toward how the Society functions. His curiosity is timed to a continuous rise. At the time deemed appropriate by the publisher, the invitation is given, the date is set. He tells the prospect what time he will call for him. He is assured that there will be no need to feel self-conscious or awkward about entering a strange building and being in a place where everybody knows everybody else except the newcomer. The Witness knows that the prospect is likely to feel out of place. He will remember back to the evening when he was in a similar situation, and keeps all this in mind as he introduces him around.

There is no need for the newcomer to feel uncomfortable or apprehensive. These people have been extremely well instructed in the art of hospitality. They have learned how to put a person at ease by giving him just the right amount of attention to bring his guard down, relax him, and make him feel at home with them. He is helped to sense that these are "his kind of people." Everyone is friendly. There is no air of forced pleasantness whatever. They are genuinely interested in meeting and talking with both visitors and prospects. Nothing is contrived. No stage is set beyond the display of good manners required of Witnesses. The atmosphere is informal without straining at it self-consciously. The Witnesses regard each other as God's chosen people, so that's that. It helps to make it easy to accept the outsider when he is the guest in your home, Kingdom Hall.

After meeting the person who is the selected head of the congregation, and who presides at the meetings, the prospect-guest is shown around the small hall. He has already been introduced to many of the faithful. On one wall his attention may have been directed to what is called a "congregation chart." This records the number of house-to-house canvass calls made each month. By reading it one may determine the number of hours that have been used in house calls, the number of contacts made, the number of return or back calls made. The number of magazines and pieces of appropriate literature that have been "placed" are also recorded. (The word "sold" is not used. This is understandable, for they do not consider themselves a business but an "enterprise," with Jehovah at the head of it. Yet, the external aspects of the Society's headquarters in Brooklyn give the impression that the Witnesses are a publishing house first.)

The prospect discovers that the Society sets a quota for each phase of the work. The results are sent annually to the head office. There is among the quotas an expectancy of the number of hours that each person should spend in making the house-to-house canvass, how many home Bible study courses he should conduct, the number of back calls persistently made, as well as the total figures of how many magazines, books, and pamphlets have been distributed. What the prospect finds out at a later date is that each man is expected to meet these quotas each month if he expects to be given any responsible position in the congregation. Most Witnesses naturally and rightly aspire to such distinction.

There is much detail work in such an operation, so several assistants are needed. Somebody must be responsible for gathering together the reports on the house calls. They must be compiled and the results sent regularly to the head office. The reports on all the home Bible study courses are also assembled and dealt with in like manner. In this way the Society always knows in any congregation exactly how many times the study has been held each month in each home where this is in progress. The number of persons attending is recorded, even the name of each publication.

Several persons are required to handle the literature, the magazines, booklets, and books, and the keeping of these accounts. An area map marked off into territories is kept current so that every phase of the operation is properly kept track of. The title "servant" is most commonly used because it is in keeping with the spirit of the New Testament, the relationship between Jesus and His friends, and portrayed as well by Him in so many of the parables that He told. ("Well done, thou good and faithful servant.")

Special use is made of a verse from Matthew:

> But the greatest one among you must be your
> minister.
>
> —Matthew 23:11, NWT

The whole program is run with business-like efficiency. All things are geared to the highest possible productivity with a minimum of lost time, money, or manpower. They compare themselves, not especially to the bee, or to the ant of Proverbs 6:6, but, characteristically, to something more complicated. They refer to the Book of Joel on the subject:

> What was left by the caterpillar, the locust has eaten; and what was left by the locust, the creeping, unwinged locust has eaten; and what the creeping, unwinged locust has left, the cockroach has eaten.
>
> —Joel 1:4, NWT

This is interpreted as referring to ways in which the Witnesses as publishers go over and over the same ground assimilating all that is good and worthwhile, thus adding righteous people to the Society.

The meeting begins with a song from the Witness songbook. The Witnesses are emphatically nonliturgical. As a result, there is no set service form or ceremonial except in the barest sense of the word, and that only so that orderly people may have an order to things in worship also. They have no prayer book or worship manual of any kind. Prayers must come from the heart, they say. They must be spontaneous. The Lord's Prayer is looked upon purely as a model, or a guide as to what and how one should pray for anything.

Only the male members present at the meetings are invited to lead in prayer. This is only one of the many ways in which the whole Society expresses its total conviction that the male of the species is superior physically, mentally, emotionally, and perhaps even spiritually. They embrace the stringent attitude of St. Paul to the letter. Paul never missed an opportunity to express and clarify man's superiority over woman. He was something of a theological bully on the subject:

> But I want you to know that the head of every man is the Christ; in turn the head of a woman is the man; in turn the head of the Christ is God.
>
> —1 Corinthians 11:3, NWT

> For man is not out of woman, but woman out of man; and, what is more, man was not created for the sake of the woman, but woman for the sake of the man.
>
> —1 Corinthians 11:8-9, NWT

> Let wives be in subjection to their husbands as to the Lord, because a husband is head of his wife as the Christ also is head of the congregation, he being a savior of this body.
>
> —Ephesians 5:22-23, NWT

These passages are accepted as literally as any other passages from Scripture. They are literally carried into the policy and practice of the Society. The organization is completely run by men. It was organized by men. Women have no positions of authority in the movement except in the rare situation where there are no male members of a tiny congregation. (This is a condition that is becoming rarer every day.) In such a situation where a woman is appointed *by the Society headquarters* to preside at meetings, she is instructed, as St. Paul demanded, to keep her head covered at all times to remind herself that she is fulfilling a position that rightfully belongs to a man and will be surrendered to him as soon as one is baptized and received into the congregation. There is not the slightest trace of Women's Liberation in the Society. There isn't even a slight groundswell. Going a step further, if a man in the congregation is considered "hen-pecked" or unduly influenced by his wife, he will be removed from office upon a report to Bethel. This is usually accomplished through failure to be reappointed by the head office in Brooklyn when the complaint has finally trickled up to the men in charge of such unfortunate matters.

Not much time is lost at Kingdom Hall meetings in either prayer or singing. They get down to the business of the meeting almost at once. This means studying the lead article of the most recent issue of *The Watchtower*. This is done in the same way that the home Bible study is done. The practice of many persons is to underline the key sentence in each article of the *Watchtower* before coming to meeting. This way, whenever one is called upon, he may refer directly to the passage, although he is always encouraged to put the thought into his own words. When one continues in this practice for awhile, the Society's thoughts soon become the individual Witness's own. It is hard to tell where one leaves off and the other begins.

The newcomer finds out very soon that Witnesses are expected to attend several meetings each week. Without exception, meetings are neatly programmed to last exactly one hour. Everything is in order. Going to four or five meetings a week of different kinds is simply taking St. Paul's injunction literally:

> Not forsaking the gathering of ourselves together, as some have the custom, but encouraging one another, and all the more so as you behold the day drawing near.
>
> —Hebrews 10:25, NWT

Absenteeism is a sure and certain sign of lethargy to the Witness. It is sometimes pointed out that Christ never misses a meeting. It is therefore an act of disrespect to Him not to be present when He is there. Naturally enough, there is Scriptural justification for this, too:

> For where there are two or three gathered together in my name, there I am in their midst.
> —Matthew 18:20, NWT

In this way every Witness is committed to learning the faith and developing the skills to articulate it in his house-to-house ministry as a publisher.

The prospect may be surprised to see so many young children in attendance. They are brought to the meetings on the grounds that the Israelites took their children with them to hear the law of Jehovah expounded by Moses:

> Congregate the people, the men and the women and the little ones and your alien resident who is within your gates, in order that they may listen and in order that they may learn, as they must fear Jehovah your God and take care to carry out all the words of this law.
> —Deuteronomy 31:12, NWT

and

> Now people began bringing him young children for him to touch these; but the disciples reprimanded them. At seeing this Jesus was indignant and said to them: "Let the young children come to me; do not try to stop them, for the kingdom of God belongs to suchlike ones."
> —Mark 10:13-14, NWT

Children are not supposed to use crayons or to write or

scribble during the meetings. They must pay attention. Side attractions are frankly condemned. There are certain loopholes, however. There is one instance where a creative approach was used in dealing with the problem. During a meeting, each child was told to count and mark down the number of times the word "Jehovah" was spoken. At the end of the meeting, it was then determined which child came the closest to the correct total. (One presumes that an adult Witness also kept a tally to determine the right answer.)

There are no arrangements for religious education other than the meetings, as far as children are concerned. There is not any Sunday School or classes of any kind for them. For the Witnesses, the reason is quite sound. There weren't any Sunday Schools in ancient Israel. Indeed, there weren't any in Christian Churches until about a hundred and fifty years ago. The whole concept is regarded as ephemeral, modern, sophisticated, and unworkable. The retort frequently is, "What does Sunday School accomplish today where it is still operating?" They have a point there. Consistently, there are no nurseries or playrooms for those of more tender years. There will be no deflecting of future Witnesses into a soundproof playroom.

Through adhering to this rigid practice, it is believed that the child first learns by being obedient. Gradually, by being with adults, and being required to be quiet, he begins to pick up bits of information. But what the Witness, either on the local congregational level or on the administrative and management levels, prefers *not* to look at is the frightening percentage of revolt from the Society by teenagers and young adults. By the time these are free from parental controls and family customs, they take off, having had quite enough of the business. In a sense, this is generally true of any person who has been born and raised in a tradition. Note the early experiences of the first two leaders of the Witnesses. Pastor Russell departed from the Presbyterian Church of his childhood, principally on the grounds of the hell-fire-and-brimstone concept of hell that was promoted in that generation in Allegheny, Pennsylvania. Judge Rutherford was raised in a stern and austere Baptist faith of the 1880s in Missouri. In a way, they both became what they attempted to escape, but the revolt was there. The third leader, Nathan Knorr, left the church of his fathers, along with his family, during his high school days, presumably because they felt they were not being fed spiritually. That the reaction to a rigid custom and practice is severe and total generally is true in any generation; it is painfully and specifically true in the case of the present one.

One night is set aside each week for Group Study. This is a session devoted to going over the more recent publications of the Society, be they books or pamphlets. More often than not, these meetings are held in homes with groups numbering from three or four up to sometimes a dozen. It is usually from such groups that the house-to-house work is organized. It is a practical approach inasmuch as those who are meeting together for advanced study are all from the same immediate neighborhood. In this way a segment of the congregation works better and more efficiently than the larger whole. Everyone's personal circumstances can be taken into consideration in the call assignments and the territory to be covered.

The men, especially, have jobs that take up their time (and the women increasingly so in these days); but the Witness considers his job solely as a means of paying living expenses; it is for the care, feeding, clothing, and sheltering of his family. Invariably he gives his energies and dedication to his employer as his just due. Everything else he gives to God. No community involvements for him. No school boards or activities, no service clubs, no special interest groups or patriotic organizations. He will have no part of anybody else's karma or the paying of their personal debt to the Law. There is no idle time for hobbies or television for the Witness. He has more important things to do. He is headed toward Armageddon and the new Eden. His faith and belief are total and beyond question. His religion is a total life style, as was that of the Christian in the primitive Church. His commitment and involvement with the secular world, his job and his neighborhood end right there. He gives his due and that's it.

Besides the time spent in house-to-house canvassing, the conduct of the home Bible study appointments, the group study sessions to keep up with Witness literature, plus the record-keeping and the administrative detail that is involved, there is also the Theocratic Ministry School to operate.

This is a local congregation version of Bethel School and is an excellent reflection of it. Even on the local congregational level, every Witness is trained in the basic principles of public speaking, personality projection, and personal grooming. Everybody is enrolled in the school. Included in the agenda is the ordeal of taking one's turn speaking on a subject for eight minutes to an audience made up of his colleagues. When he finishes his talk, he is counseled by the leader, the Ministry School "Servant," on how he could improve. The textbook for such a course contains practical suggestions on how to improve one's public speaking. It is called "Qualified to be Ministers." It is an excellent publication.

These people truly labor over voice projection, stance, poise, and proper diaphragm breathing. Through this method, even a semi-literate person, or one with a limited educational background, can be turned into an articulate speaker and worthy emissary of Jehovah.

The Society has run into a slight dilemma. There are

so many more women in the organization than there are
men that they are included as members of the Ministry
School. So many of the house calls are made when the men
are at work that women soon become dominant. They have
proven to be useful to the Society and well-nigh indispensable in getting the house-to-house canvassing accomplished. The snag, as one might suspect, is Paul's instruction to Timothy:

> I do not permit a woman to teach, or to exercise
> authority over a man, but to be in silence.
> —1 Timothy 2:12, NWT

The Witnesses are not only literal-minded in their
approach to Scripture; they are also highly practical people. When they came to realize that women do the bulk of
the calling work, anyway, they decided that women need
training in it even more than the men do. However, in their
training they are not allowed to address the audience
directly, as if they were teaching, but must present their
arguments to another woman who is in the learning group.
They work up a little psychodrama, sometimes. That is, a
scene is acted out on the doorstep of a prospect. One
woman takes the part of the householder and the other person takes the part of the publisher. Thus, they have
rationalized themselves around Paul's order to Timothy,
(and the succeeding generations of the faithful), and have
found a way across this mined field of male chauvinism.

This psychodrama technique—the Witness version of
sensitivity training—is also used at their Service Meetings.
These are designed on the order of the above in the re-crea-
tion of scenes and situations in which the publisher may
find himself (or herself), in the course of calling and of conducting the home Bible study. They are somewhat on the
order of a sales meeting, except that time is not spent on

explaining and extolling the merits of the merchandise. Jehovah does not need this. However, time here is spent on the art of hospitality. These demonstrations are also acted out.

Characters are selected to be up front as silent role-players. The rest of the class watch what's going on. The tape recorder is started and the dialogue begins. The "actors" move about according to direction. Sometimes they pretend to be saying the words, on the order of present-day television commercials in which the action is filmed complete with the mouthing of the words, which are later recorded under controlled conditions to remove interference. Then the two are later synchronized. Give the Witnesses credit. They used the technique long before Madison Avenue ran it up the flagpole to see if anybody would salute it. The Witness training school also puts the cookies on the lower shelf for the learners.

The lives of these people are filled with meetings and going about into the homes of people to whom they would bring their message of doom and hope. They *know* that the last days are here, so it is not unbearable to sacrifice their time and energies toward this end. They are spurred on by the haunting spectre of Armageddon coming up on the horizon like the harvest moon. It is even as the small, black cloud the size of a man's hand that was reported to Elijah on Mt. Carmel in days of old. The Witnesses would like this comparison best.

Let's see how our prospect is holding up as the moments of truth, one after another (and in order), come before him for review as the days go by. After his initial experience at Kingdom Hall, the Bible study class continues in his home for awhile. He is quietly helped to understand that inasmuch as he spends so many hours a week at work in the company of the wrong kind of people, he needs an hour a day at Kingdom Hall, or in house-to-house calling, to

counteract the effect and cancel out the influence that outsiders probably have had on him. The amount of time he
spends at Kingdom Hall increases. Soon he is invited to go
along on some house calls. He is assured that he is neither
required nor expected to say anything unless he wants to
share in the Witnessing.

The publisher has also been well trained and practiced
in helping the newcomer over the hurdle. He does so with
as much tact as he can put together. The "bid" or invitation usually comes about after the Bible study has
progressed for several weeks, and there has been on this
particular occasion an especially good evening of it. The
Witness is likely, after one of these sessions, to begin talking about the work of the Society, its world-wide extent.
He may also explain in some detail the publishing end of
the Watchtower Bible and Tract Society, and *how* the
Witnesses spread the word, how the territory is
systematically and regularly covered. He is not invited to
accompany his friend on house calls until all this has been
explained to him. An appointment is made for next Sunday afternoon for him to go with his new friend, the
publisher, and see for himself how it is done.

The prospect is now prepared for his baptism of fire. He
is comforted and assured that the people he will meet on
these house-to-house calls are likely to know much less
about the Bible than he does, even though he has but
recently begun the study of Scripture himself.

I sometimes doubt whether the Witness himself is
always aware of the effect of his offensive strategy. This
planned smattering of isolated and unrelated texts throws
almost any conceivable defense into a shambles. Very few
householders have a sufficient grasp of Scripture to be able
to refute the spot-passage approach. It is because of the
failure of the orthodox mainline churches to teach their
people that the Witnesses find it so easy to out-maneuver

prospects by the polite scriptural bullying at which they have become so adept. The churches have learned to their sorrow and lament that it is next to impossible to motivate their own people to study Scripture, even though in many congregations there are weekly classes in the study of Scripture. The main body of the congregation is unaware of this and remain totally unaffected by it.

This experience usually turns out to be heady stuff for the prospect. He is now well on the way to becoming a full-fledged Witness and will soon be ready to fly with the others as they go about warning everybody in the neighborhood over and over again of the imminence of the day of Jehovah's wrath.

And so goes the course and the cause.

> Hail the Theocracy, ever increasing!
> Wondrous expansion is now taking place.
> Praise to Jehovah is sung without ceasing
> By those who walk in the light of his face.
> Long years ago saw the humble beginning
> As our Redeemer a lowly way trod.
> Now a great crowd join the "remnant" in bringing
> Praises to him at the right hand of God.
>
> —Songbook

11

The Expectancy
of the End

Living on the threshold of the millennium
can be an exciting experience—when and if you have become totally convinced of the certainty of it. The Jehovah's
Witness is one of those persons who has been persuaded
that Jehovah is about to finish His Sabbath Rest at any
moment, and will begin again to get on with creation and
make ready for the creation of the New Eden. Although the
Witnesses maintain steadfastly that it's all in the Book,
the Bible actually has almost nothing to say about the nature of life on earth after the expected Armageddon. What
it does have to say is lofty in thought, colorful in language,
and completely lacking in any specific descriptions of what
it will be like. There are no descriptions of the specific nature of the New Eden. The Witnesses have been able to
dredge up some rather vivid descriptions of the Last Days,
but not of the new days that will follow the holocaust.

It is fundamental to the beliefs of the Society that the prophecies of the end will be fulfilled imminently. That means within the almost-immediate and foreseeable future. We can examine their version of the evidence through Scripture, but for the probability of a restored Eden on earth, one has to rely entirely on what might be called the oral and written tradition of the movement. As one inquires into these matters, the awareness grows that the Society has painted itself into a corner this time. It has been there before through the "computational" errors of Pastor Russell and the energetic but wrong hunches of the late Judge Rutherford. This time the date set for Armageddon closes in—not through the efforts of a third prophet so much as by the nature of their whole system of thought.

According to Witness writings, the two forms of the evidence that bring the Society to the conclusion that the curtain is falling are chronology and prophecy. Beginning with the method of the isolated spot-passages indicating the finger of God, certain verses have been extracted and strung out on a line as laundry is lifted from the clothes basket. By reading this clothesline, a person may make a few guesses about the family life, represented by the size and nature of the wash. The Witnesses believe that they have unraveled history through interpreting the various texts that are hung out to flap in the millennial breeze.

The Witnesses claim there are thirty-nine prophetic signs of the end. They are believed to be in the final stages of fulfillment in our time. When one takes the signs, or verses, singly one cannot conclude much. But when they are lifted out of context and out of the scriptural clothes basket and strung out on the eschatological clothesline, the Witnesses insist that the evidence is overwhelmingly in favor of the view that the end of all things finally is at hand.

This list of signs is compiled in a book called *Make Sure*

of All Things. While it is true that this book was published over twenty years ago (1953), it gives one certain insights into their attempts to fit their version of biblical prophecy into the sudden shifts and changes of the present-day world. Among the signs are: world wars, widespread famines, an unusual number of earthquakes, the beginning of changes in weather patterns (caused entirely by man's tampering with nature), increased lawlessness, and moral degeneracy in public and private life. Most of the signs are a Witness application of Jesus' words in the "Little Apocalypse" recorded in Matthew 14 and Luke 21, where Jesus answers the disciples' question:

> Tell us, When will these things be, and what will
> be the sign of your presence and of the conclusion
> of the system of things?
> —Matthew 24:3, NWT

Jesus' answer is the well-known statement—reminiscent of Isaiah and other prophets—that "nation will rise against nation and kingdom against kingdom, and there will be food shortages and earthquakes in one place after another."

When one either consults a commentary on this chapter, or reads the verses for himself, one strongly suspects that Jesus was predicting the destruction of Jerusalem in 70 C.E., marking the end of the Jewish world, destroyed by the power and might of Rome. The Witnesses do admit this, but they go on to add that this prophecy has a major and minor fulfillment. The minor one is the destruction of Jerusalem. The major one is today's fulfillment in imminent Armageddon.

Even a cursory examination of the history of the Church and of Christian doctrine reveals that the Church's eschatological teachings have been soft-pedaled or complete-

ly neglected and by-passed since the close of the first century. The teachings on the four last things—Death, Judgment, Hell, and Heaven (the four keynotes of the four Sundays in Advent in the liturgical year)—have fallen into
general disuse since those days, except for their occasional
and sporadic revival in the various millennial-minded
groups down through the years.

The New Testament is filled with these eschatological
urgencies:

> Young children, it is the last hour, and, just as
> you have heard that antichrist is coming, even
> now there have come to be many antichrists,
> from which fact we gain the knowledge that it is
> the last hour.
>
> —John 2:18, NWT

> The end of all things has drawn close. Be sound
> in mind, therefore . . . .
>
> —1 Peter 4:7, NWT

The expectancy of the end was foremost in the thought of
the early Christians. After the years 95-100 C.E., the subject
fades from view and no longer holds the attention of the
early Church. The urgency disappears and the steam goes
out of the tiny, infant Church because the predicted and
anticipated end does not come to pass.

An interesting modern-day theory on the subject of the
abrupt termination of the popularity of the subject and the
concern of the people about it, does throw some light on
this mystery.

About twenty-five years ago, a book appeared that was
ridiculed and howled down by the scientific establishment
as being made up of total and complete nonsense, and contrary to all facts and all learning. Today it keeps reappear-
ing in paperback reprints. Each time it enjoys a new surge
of life, the thesis becomes easier to believe. It is this:

The stories in the Book of Exodus are literally true. The writers were attempting to put down the story of all the terrible calamities that had happened, *as* they happened and without exaggeration. Until recently this has been exceedingly difficult for modern man to digest. Such phenomena as the parting of the Red Sea, the plagues of Egypt, the fires from heaven, the volcanoes, earthquakes, and manna, have long been regarded by educated persons as exaggerations and distortions. Modern man isn't as sure about such things today. The thesis, in part, is that the earth, in her rolling through space in orbit, ran into the electromagnetic tail of a celestial body that had intersected the earth's orbit, nearly making a direct hit. The resulting near-collision produced a cataclysm from which the earth is still recovering. The effect of the resulting trauma on man is still felt in his anxieties and apprehensions over meteorological phenomena. He has been concerned about solar storms, planetary conjunctions and oppositions, comets and strange doings in the skies ever since. This particular catastrophe recorded in Exodus was possibly triggered by the explosion of the Santorini caldera in the Aegean Sea when the volcano on the island of Thera blew up and likely created the tsunami, or tidal wave, which created the withdrawal of the Red Sea waters.

The author of this unusual theory used the writings of the Old Testament as well as the ancient writings and oral traditions of the various cultures around the world. He tries to fit them together into a coherent whole. This book, *Worlds in Collision*, by Immanuel Velikovsky, develops this thesis from this beginning. He notes next that about fifty-two years later there was a lesser but still severe repeat performance during the days of Joshua and Jericho. Similar events of the same nature, though less severe, are recorded as "the commotion in the days of Uzziah" in the book of the prophet Amos, and the later destruction of

Jerusalem during the reign of Hezekiah and recounted by Isaiah. These events occurred about 750 years after the Exodus, including the fifty-year lapse between dual return visits of this "fire from whose tail streams horrendous plagues and vengeance of the Lord," according to medieval chroniclers.

The beginning of the Christian era—marked by the Nativity, or birth of Jesus—occurred during a time when the anxieties and dreads of the people were mounting. The chronologies of the time indicated that the earth was due for another visitation by this scourge from the skies led by the angels of fire and destruction. It had been about 750 years since the last terrible outburst, so a suspected cycle was beginning to be expected. These anxieties were stimulated by the appearance of the comet Typhon in 44 B.C.E. This was at the time of the ides of March when the assassination of Julius Caesar came about. The subsequent death of Cato marked the end of the Republic and the departure of Rome's last statesman. In 11 B.C.E. Halley's comet appeared in a brilliant display. Then in 6 B.C.E. a triple conjunction of three planets in the western sky at sunset really stirred things up.

This latter was apparently the "star of the east" followed to Bethlehem by the Magi. These explanations may help to open the understanding to the expectancies of those days that saturated the minds of men with fear, apprehension, and dread.

When one reads the "Little Apocalypse" against this background of information and speculation, one begins to get the idea that perhaps Jesus anticipated the end as well, but with Himself as a figure in the catastrophic last days. There is some evidence in Scripture to indicate that He may have believed that all this may come together with His death, followed by the apocalyptic vision of the new life and the new kingdom on earth that was bound to follow immediately after the resurrection. Characteristically, the true believers, or sons of God, would be the ones who would survive the holocaust.

Looking backward to the years 45-60 C.E., when the Gospels began to be compiled, there was some belief that the failure of the catastrophe to come about in 33 C.E. was due to the probability that the atoning and sacrificial death of Jesus had postponed the divine wrath until the jubilee year fifty-two years hence. "Jubilee" was used to denote a period of thanksgiving, which was originally celebrated following the lesser cataclysms of the times of Joshua and Isaiah. A lesser calamity was certainly something to jubilate about.

Doing one's eschatological arithmetic, the idea emerges that the end of all time, coming about at the expected jubilee some fifty years away from the first Pentecost, would mark the end of the world at somewhere between 85 C.E. and the turn of the century. It is precisely at this point that the eschatological hopes and expectancies of the time disappear from the minds of the faithful. The days of the fateful crisis came and went, and nothing happened to indicate that the scroll of time was about to roll up. There were no more celestial fireworks warning of the impending doom. According to Velikovsky, what happened during the time of Isaiah was that the celestial body that had created such frightful havoc went roaring off into space and into a planetary orbit around the sun, to this day still slowing down in its clockwise rotation, opposite to the other planets in the solar system. Not having any way of knowing this, man's anxiety and dread naturally mounted as the days were ticked off and the anniversary of the first cataclysm came about. This may be why the faithful were waiting for the return of the Lord with His avenging angels of fire.

Although every generation has experienced earthquakes,

wars, famines, and plagues, still there have been none to compare in magnitude with those recorded in the Hebrew Scriptures. However, lacking a comprehensive grasp of the flow of time in history, the Witness approach is frequently one of statistics in which it is pointed out that the increase in catastrophes has been going on since 1914 on a scale heretofore unknown in the history of humanity since scriptural days.

However, it would appear that the main difference between the eschatological thinking of the first-century Christians and the twentieth-century Jehovah's Witnesses is that the early church had the ringing note of triumph in their expectancies. They did not thrive so much on the sufferings of first-century times as they did on spreading the good news, the Gospel, that there was a way out. This was variously described as "putting on the Lord Jesus Christ," thus being saved from the endless round of human existence. To become a Christian in those days meant accepting baptism, "donning the Lord Jesus Christ," spinning off the wheel of earthly life and becoming a king, receiving his "unsearchable riches" and being given the power to *become* one of the Sons of God. These hopes and aspirations were inherent in the term "Gospel" in those days.

In contrast, the Jehovah's Witnesses lean heavily on the bleak side of life to support their belief that the end of all time is at hand. They believe in the *devolution* of man. They believe that man's story since Adam has been one long, downhill regression and deterioration, and that each generation has been successively more evil than the last, to the point where even the patience of Jehovah has worn itself out. The interesting theory that the divine experiment failed and the Incarnation saved the day has never been entertained by the Witnesses as a possibility.

They believe that they are the last members of humanity, having been born right at the time when the clock of time has run down and is about to stop. After Armageddon Jehovah will wind it up again. This next time Satan will not have an opportunity to tinker with the mechanism and set off another chain reaction of sin and evil that has characterized man's life since Eden.

The Witness belief that history is nothing more than the story of man's continuous descent into lower and lower levels of quality is unique among religions. The Witnesses see little in man to remind them of man's original glory as the crown of creation. This is the opposite of Darwinism, be it biological or social in its application. The steam has gone out of the Witness opposition to the Darwinian theory in our day because of the advancement of learning beyond the original thesis.

There is another wilderness to gaze at for a moment. It is another of the thirty-nine signs of the Last Days. The one in question now is the "Formation of the League of Nations and the United Nations to stand in the place of the Established Kingdom of God." Opposition of the Witnesses is of such intensity that they have, as usual, resorted to Scripture to articulate their scorn for such a business:

> And I caught sight of a woman sitting upon a scarlet-colored wild beast that was full of blasphemous names and that had seven heads and ten horns. And the woman was arrayed in purple and scarlet, and was adorned with gold and precious stones and pearls and had in her hand a golden cup that was full of disgusting things and the unclean things of her fornication. And upon her forehead was written a name, a mystery: "Babylon the Great, the mother of the harlots and of the disgusting things of the earth."
>
> —Revelation 17:3-5, NWT

The Witness interpretation of these verses begins with the identifying of the wild beast as the United Nations. (It used to be the League of Nations that was the wild beast in Judge Rutherford's heyday.) The woman is identified as "Organized Religion." Although it is not clear, there is some association in the Society between the Roman Catholic Church and the United Nations, it is asserted that the UN is subject to "religious influence." Apparently the reasoning behind all this kind of thinking is that the Kingdom of God was set up in 1914 with nobody knowing about it except members of the Society. They insist that the nations owe their allegiance to this Kingdom and sooner or later must submit their sovereignty and power to it. The Witnesses consistently claim that any organization that attempts to unite nations is nothing more than a man-made substitute for God's kingdom. They delight in pointing out how unworkable the whole idea of the UN is to them.

The Witnesses understandably love to quote the words of the Council of the Federation of Churches of Christ in America (now known as the National Council of Churches), which trumpeted the gospel that the League of Nations is "the political expression of the Kingdom of God on earth." This quotation has been raised to the level of the first of the seven classical expressions of irony and humor. They love it. This was the last word in blasphemy. The end of the road has finally been reached with such political and literary nonsense. Now, on to Armageddon!

The United Nations is regarded as the eighth world power, having succeeded the empires of Egypt, Assyria, Babylon, Persia, Greece, Rome, and the "Anglo-American combine." This eighth power, even according to Scripture, is regarded as one of the seven and is considered the final combination of all of them; hence one can make room for one more empire than Scripture literally allowed for. This part of the seventeenth chapter of Revelation is dragged into the fray:

> And the wild beast that was but is not, it is also itself an eighth king, but springs from the seven, and it goes off into destruction.
>
> —Revelation 17:11, NWT

This is currently taken to mean the resurrection of the League of Nations into the United Nations.

The Witnesses sincerely believe and accept the idea that they are members of the only truly and divinely appointed organization for the salvation of that portion of mankind that still has ears to hear, and will listen. From this position, it easily follows that all other positions must be false. When one can get to this position in his personal convictions and beliefs, then he discovers within himself a sensation of power and energy that encourages him to defend himself as he is. He comes to look upon himself as now containing all things necessary to cope with a hostile society, a species gone mad, and somehow keep his own balance. By embracing such doctrines, one can now look upon oneself as excellent and complete. This conveniently shuts him off from the necessity of listening to anybody else on any topic, except of course, those handed down in the weekly Witness study material for congregational digestion.

An outsider can be tolerated only as long as the Witness thinks there is a bare possibility that he may "turn from his wickedness and live," that he may have a change of heart, convert to the Society, and be embraced by the fellowship. The Witness has within himself some rather subtle and intimate feelings of power and superiority that urge him to a certain kind of polite condescension toward anybody who is not like he is. He imposes his own views without reserve or regard for others. These things make it possible for him to adjust to a society that has become so technological and complicated that hardly anybody can cope any longer. The Witness is an early drop-out. Although many of us secretly feel that he may have done the right thing for himself and his own sanity, still there must be somewhere a better set of reasons for doing it than a millennial dream.

The outsider, the non-Witness, wonders how such flimsy evidence could possibly convince an intelligent person of the Witness version of truth. What is often not understood is that in times of social crisis (such as humanity has been experiencing for more than a generation), these social changes, so sudden and traumatic, produce more and more material for the doom prophets to feed upon.

A whole social order today is bewildered by the speed with which man has learned and exploited the secrets of nuclear power, the development of space exploration, and the general shaking of the foundations of humanity. These fears and phobias, and the feelings of inadequacy that are the common lot of humanity now, are skillfully played upon by the Witnesses. Unless one has thought through for himself his relationship to all that is roaring around inside and outside his own life, then he is a crippled prey for such teaching. A man's faint-heartedness is exploited by the Witness, who has been served up Scripture verses to fit the situation in which all other men find themselves today.

The Witness view toward the world today is strongly reminiscent of the ancient Hebrew reaction to the Chaldean civilization in the days of Abraham. The patriarch, plodding along on the dusty plain seeking a land where he might settle down with his family and goods, went around the big city. He would not enter. He avoided being in the neighborhood of a ziggurat, a seven-story tower spiralling upwards above the haze of sun and dust so that the movements of the heavens may be noted and observed. He regarded the ziggurat as an invasion of Jehovah's privacy. As soon as Jehovah God realized that He was being spied upon, He broke up their language so that they could not even communicate with one another, nor be able to tell what they had seen. The Witness can use this analogy of the tower of Babel with considerable force. It not only shows up in our politics but in the weather reports, which are filled with equivocal double-talk, too.

In Revelation 11:18 the Bible shows that God will "destroy them which destroy the earth" (King James Version). One cannot help but have the vagrant thought that God doesn't have to bother to do so. Man is not only quite capable of doing it on his own, but is considerably advanced in his methods of accomplishing it. Even so, the remnant will move in, Jehovah will create the new Eden, the Witnesses will complete it, and the Kingdom will have been ushered in.

Another one of the signs of the Last Days is "men becoming faint out of world-wide fear." If a person has not become faint from fear yet, let him consider this text, which the Witness uses as a bludgeon:

> And the wine press was trodden outside the city, and blood came out of the wine press as high up as the bridles of the horses, for a distance of a thousand six hundred furlongs [about 200 miles].
> —Revelation 14:20, NWT

12

The Approaching Doom

There is a vivid blow-by-blow description of Armageddon contained in a Witness book for children. It is called *From Paradise Lost to Paradise Regained.* This book often has been offered for sale prior to the Christmas season, a holiday the Witnesses themselves neither celebrate nor recognize for themselves. The book is promoted as a gift for children. That's a bit of shrewdness in timing and hitting a market. Many parents and god-parents are prone to express a bit of personal piety at the Christmas season, and see to it that the child also receives "something religious" as a gift.

A glance through this slightly oversize book brightly bound in orange with gold lettering, and having a bas relief imprint of the Witness version of paradise both lost and regained, is printed in large type and has many pictures. It gives a first and fleeting impression that it is so easy to read that it can be read with positive pleasure, especially

by children. But when you take a second look at it, you
may be upset and even horrified by the way it presents the
subject of Armageddon, the favorite (and only) subject of
the Witnesses.

> Great will be the terror at Armageddon. Every
> kind of thing will be used to destroy this evil
> world. There will be cloudbursts, floods and
> lashing rains, earthquakes, giant hailstones and
> a rain of fire. There will be terror on the land,
> terror in the sea and in the air. So terrified will
> people be that they will begin killing one
> another.

The book of Zechariah is quoted:

> There will be a rotting away of one's flesh, while
> one is standing upon one's feet; and one's very
> eyes will rot away in their sockets, and one's very
> tongue will rot away in one's mouth.
>   —Zechariah 14:12, NWT

The description continues from this children's book:

> Eaten up will be the tongues of those who scoffed
> and laughed at the warning of Armageddon!
> Eaten up will be the eyes of those who refused to
> see the 'time of the end.' Eaten up will be the
> flesh of those who would not learn that the living
> and true God is named Jehovah! Eaten up while
> they stand on their feet!

Alongside this scary description—which should enhance
the fantasy and nightmare life of your favorite nephew or
granddaughter—is a full-page picture of what the God
Jehovah is going to do to everybody except the true

believer, the Jehovah's Witness. The picture shows buildings collapsing, people drowning, houses on fire, and men killing each other. The earth has opened up and there is a huge canyon. People are falling into it as into a huge and hungry maw. One can see a car and a bicycle dropping into the abyss. Following these things into the pit goes someone's front porch, railing and all. God appears as a cruel and sadistic fiend, providing nightmare fare for weeks. The text goes on:

> Worms will not stop swarming over millions of bodies until the last body is eaten up. Birds and beasts will eat their fill of human flesh until nothing is left but white bones.

Nor is that all that is described to the kiddies in this holiday gift. We learn further that the survivors (Witnesses *only*), will spend the first seven months after the holocaust burying all the bones, this in fulfillment of the passage in Ezekiel:

> And those of the house of Israel will have to bury them for the purpose of cleansing the land, for seven months . . . in the Valley of Gog's Crowd.
>
> —Ezekiel 39:12-15

This means, of course, that the mighty God Jehovah will destroy all of the human race except the Witness remnant who will be saved to make the fresh start. The final curse that is made plain is that anyone who dies at Armageddon cannot be resurrected. He is forever destroyed. Those who survive, we are now informed, "will go forth to look upon the slain of Jehovah, the surviving sheep of the New World Society."

What about the real troublemakers, the ones who brought these terrible things to pass? What will happen to the devil and his demons? Christ comes down out of heaven with a key and a chain and He ties up old Satan for a thousand years and throws him into the abyss. Then he throws all the demons in there, too. The writer explains that the abyss is a deathlike state of inactivity where Jesus Himself went for the three days between the crucifixion and the resurrection. Armageddon is over. The troublemakers have been vanquished. The nations are gone. The wicked people are gone. The new world begins!

The book concludes with a complete index to Scriptures cited: by actual count, seven hundred verses from the Bible.

> Since the days of Eden men have been searching for the PATHWAY TO PARADISE. Through the pages of this book you have followed that search. But you should not stop now. If you hope to enter that land of promise you must continue on the road to the very end. You have seen from the lives of such faithful men as Noah, Abraham, Daniel and the disciples of Jesus that it is not an easy road. Jesus Himself, by his words and deeds, made that fact quite clear. He said, "Narrow is the gate and cramped the road leading off into life, and few are the ones finding it." Will you be earnest enough to stay on that road now that you have found it? It is everlasting life that lies before you.

So reads the parting words of the book *Paradise Lost and Paradise Regained.*

The Witnesses also have books and booklets for modern men and women of various interests. The field of statistics is painstakingly utilized in order to add further weight and validity to the accumulating evidence of approaching Armageddon. We are informed by them that the First World

War was seven times more costly in lives and property than all of the nine hundred and one wars combined that have occurred in the past twenty-five hundred years. They have determined through their statisticians that the Second World War was four times as costly as the first. Since the time of the beginning of Jesus' reign in heaven in 1914, more than twice the number of people have suffered from food shortages as the sum total of people during the preceding nine hundred years.

These cheerless charts, hopeful only for the sudden and rapid end to both suffering and time, also report that since 1914, earthquakes have taken a toll of over a million lives, leaving at least twenty million homeless. These increasing numbers of disturbances clearly indicate to them the approaching doom for all unbelievers. Calamity is good news. It means that the end of suffering for everyone is at last in sight. For the unbeliever, it means the eternal sleep of death. For the Witness, it means an unending life on earth in the restored Eden:

> They are not fearful of things occurring in the old world. They are not disturbed because of the thickening darkness, the encircling cloud that surrounds and perplexes all nations. They are not afraid of wars or rumors of wars. The reason: They have hope. They *know* the outcome.

So writes a former member of Jehovah's Witnesses. The guiding Gospel motto of the Witnesses is from Matthew:

> And this good news of the kingdom will be preached in all the inhabited earth for a witness to all the nations; and then the end will come.
> —Matthew 24:14, NWT

To the Witness, this verse from Scripture is being fulfilled daily, inch by inch and step by step as each individual door is rapped, every doorbell pushed, and each piece of literature placed into the hands of an unbeliever. This alone might save one more innocent victim from the impending holocaust and cataclysm that is on Jehovah's calendar for the days ahead. Each step and each act for Jehovah brings Armageddon that much closer to happening.

13

A Convention of Martyrs

The 1974 Annual Divine Purpose Assembly of Jehovah's Witnesses for the New York area was held at Aqueduct Racetrack, on a humid weekend in August. The racetrack crowd were upstate at the races at Saratoga, so 16,000 Witnesses had the park to themselves. Those who have never been to the "Big A," or any other large racetrack, may not be aware of the park-and-garden setting of such public playgrounds, the carefully tended flower beds, and the beautifully tonsured lawns. The setting seemed to be more appropriate and congenial to the Edenic hopes of the Witnesses than to the daily double addicts. Having seen both crowds, I cannot but be impressed with the tremendous gulf between the two. On racing days one almost wades through a paper snowstorm of cast-off betting slips and disappointed hopes. That day there were signs everywhere that reminded, "If it's on the floor, pick it up." There was not so much as a gum wrapper lying about.

This phenomenon is all the more impressive when one realizes that over ten thousand chicken dinners were served in a two-hour period. The evidence was in the trash cans. The grounds and the floors were spotless—and these people were there with their children, infants and all!

Walking from the parking lot to the grandstand, I counted over fifty chartered buses. Just outside the entrance to the grandstand, there was a large above-ground swimming pool. Baptisms were going on at the time, 475 of them, brothers and sisters in Jehovah. Carol and Frank Martin were among those baptized. "We have been studying the Bible and doing field ministry for months. We have been waiting for today," Frank commented. Mrs. Martin was wearing a maternity swimsuit and said she felt as though her baptism counted for two. "Our child is dedicated to Jehovah even before his birth." Frank, the expectant father, added, "Once he's born he'll be raised by the statutes of Jehovah."

"I'm Gloria," she answered as she climbed out of the pool. The baptismal water was mixed with tears on her happy face. "I'm in a daze," she cried. "It's so wonderful to be dedicated to something like this."

Gary came by dripping wet and wearing cut-off jeans and a T-shirt. His comment to me was, "If you knew what I know about Jehovah's plan, you'd be standing here dripping and I'd be asking the questions."

When it was all over, a voice came over the loudspeaker system, "You acknowledge Jehovah to be your owner, and henceforth you will live to do His will, not your own." The several thousand applauded and cheered the message.

As the last person came down the steps from the pool, a Witness beside me who had been listening to my conversations confided that this last one has been in and out of her Kingdom Hall for ten years. "She would come into the Truth for awhile and then go back to wearing miniskirts on the street. Now she's finally come home to Jehovah." She excused herself and made her way to her friend. They walked off together, arm in arm.

It was a strange feeling to enter the huge foyer, the space under the stands where the betting windows were. In each window there were Witness tracts. Some of the betting areas were roped off for special functions. One whole section was set apart for sign-making. There were four sign-letterers working. One of them was finishing a large sign announcing where to sign up to help with the clean-up after the assembly adjourned. Another section was roped off for medical care, complete with a staff of doctors and nurses. Another large sign arrowed where the hard-of-hearing and the deaf should go for the translations of the assembly addresses. There was also a special section for Witnesses confined to wheelchairs. Everything had been taken into consideration and arranged for. Rows of tables three hundred feet long were of two different heights so that everybody could be comfortable for stand-up eating.

While standing around and absorbing the apotheosis of the gambling hall, I started a conversation with a uniformed man with the letters N.Y.R.A. on his hat, standing for New York Racing Association. "Not even a day off for you when there's no racing," I commented.

"I'm a Witness anyway," he answered. Then he went on, "All ten of us on duty belong. We volunteered for the assignment."

I was impressed, not only with ten guards and security police officers being Witnesses on duty, but the fact that there were only ten cops for 16,000 people. I told him so.

"Actually, it's rather dull. All we're here to do is to stand at the gates and watch for the nut who might come in and think he's doing Jehovah's will by shooting up the place. In a crowd like this, they're pretty easy to spot."

"Well, I must say this crowd is a strong contrast to the

ones on racing days," I said. "For one thing, the place is clean."

"When a man loses his money and his wallet, he loses his manners and then his mind," philosophized the fuzz. "When the gamblers leave, the place is a mess. They take their inward disorder along with them. Witnesses don't have any." End of interview and conversation.

Taking the escalator to the second level of the grandstand, I walked out to the bank and tier of seats, seating myself on an end seat, trying to be as inconspicuous as possible because an address was being delivered. The speaker was being listened to, as well. In front of the platform there was a huge model of an open Bible on which was written:

> He shall judge between the nations and shall decide for many peoples; and they shall beat their swords into plowshares and their spears into pruning hooks. Nations shall not lift up sword against nation, neither shall they learn war any more.
>
> —Isaiah 2:4

The speaker went on to say that we cannot truly know the exact date of the end, for that is presuming to know the thoughts of Jehovah, and that is contrary to Scripture. Then he quoted Isaiah 55:8:

> "For my thoughts are not your thoughts, neither are your ways my ways," says the Lord.

He ended with the words, "Don't second-guess Jehovah."

The applause was thunderous and long. I gazed around the entire grandstand holding the sixteen thousand, about evenly divided between white, black, and Latin people.

The young woman next to me, whom I judged to be in

her mid-thirties, was laughing while the tears ran down her cheeks. She turned to me and smiled. "Wasn't that wonderful?" she beamed. "I still think the end is very soon, though."

"What makes you think that?" I asked quietly.

"I have leukemia," she explained. "I have it now, but I won't have it for very long."

Thinking that she meant that she was suffering from an advanced state of that curse, I commented that blood transfusions were out of the question for her because of her convictions.

"Oh yes, of course," she replied. "But that isn't a problem. I guess you could say that Jehovah holds the cure for cancer. I'll get my health back one way or the other through my death and resurrection in Jehovah, or perhaps I'll still be around at Armageddon. And I think I shall," she concluded.

I found myself agreeing with her at the moment, only to be divided inwardly again as I was waiting to go down the escalator. My inner turmoil returned when a person for whom I stood aside said:

"Wasn't that a marvelous speech?" Not waiting for my agreement, she went on. "This is my third assembly and that's the best address yet."

I picked her up on this, inasmuch as her mild euphoria made her chatty. "How soon do you think Armageddon will begin?" I asked.

"The political upheavals in every nation signal that it is about to start. Jehovah has had enough and He is going to vindicate Himself within this next year. Look what His anger has done to the churches!"

I encouraged her to go on.

"Well, I was a Catholic nun for eleven years, and then one day a nice man handed me a copy of *Awake!* and I read it. I was surprised to find out that Jesus wasn't crucified but was executed on a stake. All those years in the Church, and they hadn't told me! So that was that, as far as I'm concerned. That was a real close call for me. Just think, what if I'd never met that person on the street corner!"

That day my understanding was truly opened. Now I perceive the kind and degree of faith and conviction that it takes to outlast all adversity. What I witnessed was an example of the kind of faith and practice that it takes to survive in an alien and hostile society. Not since the persecution of the Mormons, over a hundred years ago, have there been such attacks upon a "peculiar" people in the United States of America. The word "peculiar" is used here in its original meaning of "unusual," "set apart," or "unique." No religious minority has ever endured as much injustice in this nation as the Witnesses have from American society.

This doesn't particularly bother the Witnesses, however. This is because they understand and believe that persecution is simply one of Satan's efforts to seduce them. They believe that he uses persecution against them as a final and desperate attempt to bring the Witnesses' efforts to nothing, realizing that he has but a short time to work. They also point out that since Satan was finally driven out of heaven in 1914, he has been able to concentrate his efforts to the earth exclusively, and that this is why their times have been harder than ever.

During World War II, over twenty-five hundred mobs in at least forty-four different states of the union violently attacked these people for one or all three of the following reasons:

(1) The Witnesses refuse either to salute the flag or even to give the Pledge of Allegiance to it. They insist that it is nothing more than a

graven image, citing the Second Commandment.

(2) They refuse to bear arms or have anything
whatever to do with any kind of weapons.
They regard this as a violation of the Sixth
Commandment.

(3) They refuse to place the state above their
beliefs, quoting the words of Jesus:

"Render unto Caesar the things that
are Caesar's and unto God the things
that are God's."

There is a similarity in the sufferings of the Witnesses and
those of the early Christian Church. In both ages, then and
now, there were unknown numbers who were locally
persecuted and harassed, hounded by local officials for ignoring various city, town, and village ordinances against
soliciting, unlawful meetings, and the like.

No matter where or to what degree they were persecuted,
they continually insisted upon their legal rights. At least
fifty-five cases have gone as far as the Supreme Court of
the United States. The Witnesses, through their lawyers,
won forty-four of these appeals. That is a respectable bat-
ting average in anybody's league. This is all the more
remarkable when one remembers that these cases were
decided back in the nineteen-twenties, thirties, and forties—long before today's civil and social rights causes
came about. Through their persecution and subsequent
carrying of their grievances to the highest court in the land,
they established the beachhead for thousands of oppressed
people. The floodgates were opened. Through the work of
the Witnesses, many people today enjoy privileges that
used to be denied to them in America. Moreover, Witness
experiences and Witness victories in the courts have made

it possible for other groups to employ Witness strategies with an immunity that the earlier Witnesses never had.

The Jehovah's Witnesses won the right for anybody and everybody to solicit from house to house. It is now possible to preach on a street corner without a license, thanks to the Witnesses. They may legally canvass apartment buildings—whether or not the owners or tenants give consent. Witnesses have even been recognized officially as ministers of an accredited religion. Thus, they are also exempt from military service. (Every Jehovah's Witness, as noted previously, is a minister simply by virtue of being a Witness). They decline to serve on juries. They neither register nor vote. They love to wrap the word "martyr" around themselves, not as a flag, but as a cloak—not in defense, but for righteousness' sake.

There is no urgency in the Christian churches. They haven't had an eschatology for over four hundred years, with the exception of the Pentecostal bodies, who certainly have it, but not with the positive urgency or vivid conviction of the Witness. There is a pathetic remnant in custom in certain Christian churches relating to all this. In the liturgical year, the four Sundays preceding Christmas—known as the Advent season—were originally the four Sundays designated for sermons and instruction on the Four Last Things: Death, Judgment, Hell, and Heaven. But how often are the four Sundays used for this purpose? How often do you hear a sermon on the subject of heaven?

No wonder the churches are flopping about like landed fish while the Witnesses swim in the sea of life. They never get caught on any kind of bait. They know something that Christians today don't seem to understand, although it is plain enough in Scripture: "The kingdom of heaven is like a net that is let down into the sea" (Mark 13:47). The Witnesses know that they are in the net and think it's great. The Christian suspects that he's in the net and he fights it.

It has been said in ages past that "the blood of the martyrs is the seed of the Church." Today it is the Jehovah's Witnesses who know this to be true in a very special sense, because these seeds mark the end of time and the beginning of eternity for them—the fulfillment of the Edenic hope and the thousand years of peace. Persecution was the cost. To them, the price was not too high.

Appendix

The Doctrine of the Jehovah's Witnesses: a Review

Much of the Witness doctrine is difficult for the layman to grasp. It is also difficult for the theologian. One hardly knows by which door to enter into their labyrinth of faith. To begin at the end and work backwards seems to be the most enlightening and understandable way of trying to see things as the Witnesses see them. In this book we have worked from both ends, and will here set down as hard core a summary as can be mustered.

Since the day Satan was ejected from heaven and thrown earthward by Michael the Archangel and his hosts, Jehovah has carefully drawn forth a hundred and forty-four thousand of their number who will be resurrected in spirit to reign in heaven as Lords over the earth. Jesus, as Michael the Archangel became known when he was incarnated into a body, has been King of Heaven since 1914. Jehovah selects those to rule in heaven on the intensity of their righteousness, beginning with Abel, the first Witness.

The members of this elite are known as "The Little Flock." They are not selected by any agency or by any special test or qualification. They simply "know" who they are.

Most, if not all, of the hundred and forty-four thousand have by now been chosen and gathered to their fathers to await that "great getting-up morning" in heaven. A Witness census a few years ago revealed that there may be twelve to fifteen thousand of the elect who are still on earth. Some of these are still in the screening process. All the remaining Witnesses who did not make it into the hundred and forty-four thousand corps of the elite for heaven will nevertheless survive Armageddon in their present physical form. They may need some repair, such as the removal of deformities or the result of chronic arthritis and the like, but then they will set about repopulating the globe until a fixed and certain number have been born. After this there will be no more births. In this way the world's population will remain constant and stable. One thing that is not clear in this idyllic scene is whether or not children will always remain children and old folks always remain old folks perpetually in their golden years playing eternal shuffleboard. We do not know yet whether or not everybody remains set and frozen in time for the thousand years or not. Presumably this has not been worked out, and is being saved for one of the surprises for everyone who is lucky enough to be among "the other sheep" who shall inherit eternal life on a renewed and rejuvenated earth.

The Witnesses, who are known everywhere as friendly and peaceable people, expect to stand aside and watch Armageddon unfold to the bitter end. Jehovah knows that they are absolutely unbending pacifists through and through. Therefore, he will not expect them to participate in the slaughter of the unbelievers. However, it is estimated according to Scripture that it will take them seven months to bury the bones and clear away the debris. Once Satan is overcome and chained up, the earth will be restored to its Edenic grandeur and pristine beauty. The millennium will be at hand, for now the thousand-year reign of Christ, having begun in 1914, has fulfilled all the conditions for the New Eden. The dead, except for the incorrigibly wicked and evil, will be raised to have one more chance at right living.

By Witness count, mankind is six thousand years old, and has produced over two hundred and fifty billion people. The lists of the fallen but reformable is impressive. It will require strict culling if the Witnesses themselves are going to have any room to move around at all, let alone do any proper and expected repopulating. For the next thousand years, those who are resurrected will serve the saved. At the end of this time, Satan, having finally wrenched himself free from his chains after a thousand year struggle to untie the knot, will once again stalk the earth trying to mess things up again and bring to nought the works of Jehovah. Those who are seduced by him will be rounded up before the mischief spreads too far. Together, with Satan, they will be hurled into the lake of fire, Gehenna, to perish forever. The meek, the faithful survivors, will at last inherit the earth.

The latest prediction for the setting in of Armageddon was determined for the year 1975. This prophecy appeared in *Awake!* magazine in October, 1966. Believing that the creative days of Genesis are 7000 years in length, and that man was created in the autumn of 5026 B.C.E., then this date, 1975, marks the beginning of the seventh "day." Thus in 1975 the thousand-year reign of Christ will be well under way and Armageddon will commence.

We can expect the immediate future to be filled

with thrilling events for those who rest their faith in God and His promises.

—*Awake!* (6 October 1966)